T3-BUV-437

Wonders of America

The Statue
of Liberty

For my grandchildren—M. D. B.

To Frank and Isobel—J. G. W.

ALADDIN PAPERBACKS
An imprint of Simon & Schuster Children's Publishing Division
1230 Avenue of the Americas, New York, NY 10020
Text copyright © 2007 by Marion Dane Bauer
Illustrations copyright © 2007 by John Wallace
All rights reserved, including the right of reproduction
in whole or in part in any form.
READY-TO-READ, ALADDIN PAPERBACKS, and related logo
are registered trademarks of Simon & Schuster, Inc.
Designed by Christopher Grassi
The text of this book was set in Century Old Style.
Manufactured in the United States of America
First Aladdin Paperbacks edition September 2007
2 4 6 8 10 9 7 5 3 1
Library of Congress Cataloging-in-Publication Data
Bauer, Marion Dane.
The Statue of Liberty / by Marion Dane Bauer ;
illustrated by John Wallace.
p. cm.—(Wonders of America) (Ready-to-read)
ISBN-13: 978-1-4169-3479-0 (pbk)
ISBN-10: 1-4169-3479-0 (pbk)
ISBN-13: 978-1-4169-3480-6 (library)
ISBN-10: 1-4169-3480-4 (library)
1. Statue of Liberty (New York, N.Y.)—History—Juvenile literature.
2. New York (N.Y.)—Buildings, structures, etc.—Juvenile literature.
I. Wallace, John, 1966– ill. II. Title.
F128.64.L6B38 2007
974.7'1—dc22
2006036917

Wonders of America

The Statue of Liberty

By **Marion Dane Bauer**

Illustrated by **John Wallace**

Ready-to-Read
ALADDIN
New York London Toronto Sydney

4

A grand lady stands in
New York Harbor.
Her name is the
Statue of Liberty.

She holds a torch high
to welcome all who come
to the United States.

The Statue of Liberty
was created by a
French sculptor,
Frederic-Auguste Bartholdi.

France gave this
beautiful statue
to the United States

to honor the friendship
between the two countries.

The people of the United States
built the pedestal
to receive the statue.

American schoolchildren gave their nickels and dimes to make a place for Lady Liberty to stand.

Statue of Liberty

The statue is made
from sheets of copper
wrapped around a
steel structure.

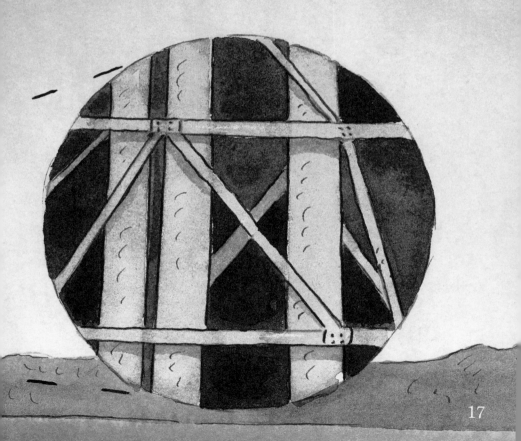

She was built in France,
then taken apart and
shipped to the United States.

When she was put
together again and
set on the pedestal,
she stood 305 feet tall.

In 1886 that was taller than
any building in New York City.

When she was unveiled
thousands of people cheered.
Ships sounded their horns
and whistles.

25

Guns saluted.

Still today the
Statue of Liberty's
torch burns bright.

It reminds all Americans
and all who come to America
that freedom lives!

Interesting Facts about the Statue of Liberty

★ The Statue of Liberty was shipped to the United States in 350 pieces. Those pieces weighed 450,000 pounds and were packed in 214 crates.

★ The statue itself, from base to torch, is 151 feet high. The arm holding the torch is 42 feet high. Lady Liberty's index finger is 8 feet long. Her mouth is 3 feet wide.

★ It has been said that Frederic-Auguste Bartholdi modeled the statue's face after his mother's.

★ Several copies of the famous statue stand in France.

★ Bartholdi's name for his statue was *Liberty Enlightening the World.*

★ Lady Liberty has welcomed more than 12 million immigrants to the United States.

★ In 1904 a bronze tablet with a poem, "The New Colossus" by Emma Lazarus, was added to a wall of the pedestal. It includes these lines:

> *Give me your tired, your poor,*
> *Your huddled masses yearning to breathe free,*
> *The wretched refuse of your teeming shore.*
> *Send these, the homeless, tempest-tost to me,*
> *I lift my lamp beside the golden door!*

T3-BUV-438

TO KANTA YAMAMOTO AND
KAZUKO ONODERA
Old Friends, Good Friends,
The Best Friends

Contents

List of Figures

List of Tables

Preface

During the past several years, while studying and teaching in universities in the United States, I have particularly engaged in research on the status attainment process. Surprisingly enough, little is known how adolescents' aspirations (or ambitions) in high school experiences influence their individual educational and occupational attainment.

A Sketch of the Book

This is an empirical study of factors influencing status attainment. In this research, I looked at a national sample of American men and women, those in the National Longitudinal Study of the High School Class of 1972, and used path analysis to estimate both the direct and the indirect effects on the educational and occupational attainment process. I extended previous work on status attainment by developing a path-analytic model that incorporates the core constructs of the two major status attainment models (the Blau-Duncan model and the Wisconsin model), and these models are representative of the two main status orientations that sociological thought has been followed.

Initially this study focused on women's attainment and therefore the proposed model for the research was adapted to reflect factors that have not been sufficiently acknowledged as affecting women's status attainment. By conducting interactive tests, however, the effect of each variable within the model was considered to be the same for men and women. Thus process is the same, yet gender can still play a role in the model because men and women may differ in constructs, but relationships among the constructs are similar for both sexes. The model was then estimated for the combined sample of men and women, and sex was included as an exogenous variable in the model.

The results of this research could be applied to today's American adolescents because the attainment process in this model estimation is found to be similar for men and women and because the attainment process for this sample is found to be similar to that of the initial Wisconsin model estimation. In sum, the results can be used for enhanced academic and career education and for counseling adolescents in the transition from high school to the adult and occupational world.

Acknowledgements

I offer my special thanks to my doctoral committee members (Drs. Horgan, Rakow, and Townsend) who guided me throughout the research and writing of my dissertation, and who critiqued my research with sensitivity and a genuine concern to enhance it; especially my sincere thanks to Dr. Ethington, my committee chair. I also want to thank Mr. and Mrs. Hellmeller and Mr. and Mrs. Amagriani, both couples were my Memphis mentors, as well as Mr. and Mrs. Tyler, my current Guam mentors, for their considerable intelligence that helped me in developing my academic and professional life. I wish to extend my appreciation to Kanta Yamamoto, my spiritual father, and Kazuko Onodera, my spiritual mother, both of them gave me the courage and tenacity to maintain high scholarly research. I would like to express my thanks to many people, including Aurora D'Amico of the Center for Education Statistics, who have contributed in many constructive ways to this research. And, of course, I want to thank all my wonderful colleagues of the University of Guam. Finally, I thank the staff of University Press of America very much and Si Yu'os Ma'ase.

Yukiko Inoue
Mangilao, Guam
November 1998

Chapter 1

Introduction

What do American young men and women give as reasons for their decision to attend college? According to Einstein (1967, 93), 64 percent of collegians surveyed gave "occupational goals, including higher income," as the most important reason for enrolling in college. A more recent survey similarly revealed that the ultimate reasons for the freshmen entering college in 1991 were "to get a better job" (79%) and "to make more money" (75%) (Astin 1993, 245). Whatever the year may be, this remains true: "Schools are the primary agencies of social selection for children and youth in the United States" (Hawser 1970, 102). Throughout American social history, indeed, one of the strongest beliefs has been that the more education people have, the better their chances for economic and occupational attainment are. The educational structure in the United States, as Woelfel (1972) has forcefully stated, is so closely intertwined with the occupational structure that it is almost impossible to discuss one without discussing the other. Thus American men and women go to college, primarily because they do wish to improve their occupational status and eventually their social status.

"Social status," as Orr (1995, 603) has identified it, "is a term used by sociologists to describe the position of an individual or a group in the hierarchical social structure." Orr has further contended that this structure encompasses the features of a society which have permanence over time, which are interrelated, and which determine both the functioning of the society and the activities of its individual members: parameters of the social structure are recognized as normative patterns, inequalities of power, and material privileges that provide members of society and their children with widely different opportunities and alternatives in the status attainment process.

Haller and Portes (1973) have identified the "status attainment process" as those sets of attainments by which individuals come to occupy their positions in the social hierarchies of wealth, power, and prestige. These three indicators are thus viewed as a set of basic "social status" dimensions. As a general rule, social status is measured by education, occupation, and income (Blau 1975) and, in general, parental socioeconomic status (hereinafter referred to as "SES") is a term used to represent the position of the entire family in the social structure of industrial societies (Dobriner 1969).

When the status system of a modern industrial society is crystallized, an adult's occupation tends to be intimately connected with his or her position in other hierarchies (Haller and Portes 1973). In Haller and Portes's words, occupational status does not exhaust the range of status variations but does appear as the most representative summary measure of the adult's social standing within the context of the modern industrial societies. This is certainly so if one restricts the field to status dimensions for which reliable measures are available.

In short, therefore, the relationship of occupational status to these specific status dimensions, as Haller and Portes (1973) have maintained, is not only evident but also pronounced, with educational attainment being regarded as primarily a determinant and with economic attainment as primarily a consequence of occupational attainment.

Problem to be Studied

Research using the 1969 Sewell-Haller-Portes (SHP) Model of Educational and Occupational Attainment Levels has resulted in an accepted and traditional understanding of the process by which American

messes Sewell,
Hauser +
Wolf (1980)

men attain their social status in the modern American society (Alwin, Otto, and Call 1976; Hauser, Tsai, and Sewell 1983; Kerckhoff and Campbell 1977). In the SHP model, of course, the key to occupational attainment is educational attainment. The bulk of the studies replicating the SHP model within the sociological context has been devoted to the status attainment process for men only: a few prominent studies are conducted by Alexander, Eckland, and Griffin (1975), Crouse and Mueser (1978), Gilbert (1977), Kerckhoff and Huff (1974), Marini (1978), Picou and Carter (1976), Porter (1974, 1976), Sewell, Haller, and Ohlendorf (1970), and Wilson and Portes (1975).

The status attainment process for American women thus needs to be more fully understood by applying social-psychological concepts to both the explanation of variation in the attainment process and the level of educational and occupational attainment. The aforementioned studies have confirmed that both parental status and parental encouragement play significant roles in the attainment process for men. Is the process by which women attain their status the same as the process by which men attain their status? In particular, does SES play a similar role for women in determining their status attainment process when examined from the same sociological perspectives as that for men?

review
and address
some
of this

Purpose of the Study

The purpose of this study was thus to estimate a variation of the SHP model for the national sample of high school seniors of 1972, the year in which Title IX of the Education Amendments was enacted. This study was an empirical attempt to determine the process by which aspirations were formed and the manner in which they influenced subsequent attainment-oriented behaviors. According to Payne and Abbott (cited in Lampard 1995), the attainment process for women is contingent on their life-cycle positions. "Historically, American women have been identified with the domestic domain of home and family" (Hayes 1986, 4), and "Women have received less encouragement to attend graduate or professional schools" (Baird 1976, 31). "While men are still expected to have one primary role (work), women are expected to combine work and family roles" (Bolig 1982, 16). Further, women who are single and have no children differ from women who are mothers (Liao and Cai 1995). Hence it follows that women's attainment process may be largely determined by their marital status and the number of children they have. Thus both marital status and the number of children were included as variables in the model for this study.

"Higher education is charged with the task of preparing men and women for high-level occupations" (Baird 1976, 20). Consequently, an undergraduate degree (credential) might be the most important event for Americans to attain such high-level occupations. More and more, however, Americans are attending graduate and professional schools because they need degrees to be able to do what they like or to earn what they deserve. Advocating the position that social origin continues to influence an individual's educational attainment after his or her childhood, Baird (1976) has asserted that the most egalitarian institutions in the United States have been colleges. In Baird's words, therefore, academic success in the United States is still largely dependent on such variables as ability, achievement, and aspiration.

In the proposed model for this study, the levels of educational and occupational aspirations were hypothesized to be the principal influences on educational and occupational attainment. Educational attainment in the Wisconsin model was operationalized as a dichotomous variable, indicating whether or not the respondent obtained an undergraduate degree. In contrast, educational attainment in this study was considered to be a continuous variable, indicating the highest academic degree the respondent obtained.

Finally, while occupational attainment was the ultimate variable in the proposed path-analytic model of this study, the primary focus of this study was on educational attainment, the factors influencing it, and its role as a moderating variable for the indirect effect on occupational attainment.

Chapter 2

Review of Literature

The first section of this chapter details the background of the research problem of this study, focusing on the two main status attainment models in American sociology. The second section provides a historical overview of women in American higher education. The third section focuses on the relationship between social origin and status attainment.

Status Attainment Models

"During the past two decades, several varieties of structural research on the status-attainment paradigms have flourished within [American] sociology" (Breiger 1995, 115). However, according to Hanson (1994), research on educational and occupational attainment in the United States has relied primarily on a functionalist socialization model, beginning with the 1967 Blau-Duncan Model of the Occupational Attainment Process of the American Adult Male Population (well known as the "Occupational Stratification Model," or simply the "Blau-Duncan

Model") and continuing in the aforementioned 1969 SHP model (well known as the "Wisconsin Social-Psychological Model of Status Attainment," or simply the "Wisconsin Model"). That is to say, "The Blau-Duncan and Wisconsin models are representative of the two main status-attainment orientations that sociological thought has followed" (Haller and Portes 1973, 56).

The Blau-Duncan Model

This model was first estimated for American adult male samples derived from the Current Population Survey of 1962. The Blau-Duncan model has been best known among causal theories of status attainment in American sociology; indeed, its focus was on the structure of status transmission. Blau and Duncan (1967) made an attempt to reconceptualize the classic questions of the mobility research which had concentrated on (1) the extent to which ascriptive factors at birth would determine subsequent attainment levels and (2) the extent to which initial positions of individuals in the stratification system would influence their social positions at later points in time. Blau and Duncan's conceptualization is portrayed in a path model (see Figure 2.1): in the model, the straight lines stand for causal paths theoretically expected, whereas the curved line represents the unanalyzed correlation between variables that are not assigned causal priority.

The 1969 Blau-Duncan model has basically posited the following: (1) although the father's position in the social structure exercises some significant direct influence, its primary impact on the son's occupational attainment is indirect through the son's educational attainment level; and (2) the son's educational attainment level is one that does exert an influence on his first and current occupational status, while his first occupational status has a sizable effect on his current occupational status. These suppositions definitely imply Hauser's (1970, 104) theorized notion: "Stratification is a process, not a state. The relationships between social origin and academic performance in educational systems develop over a period of years, as do those between educational performance and adult achievement."

The estimation of the Blau-Duncan model thus provided considerable evidence of the influence of the father's social standing (measured both by his occupational status on the basis of income and prestige and by his educational level) on the son's occupational attainment, strongly

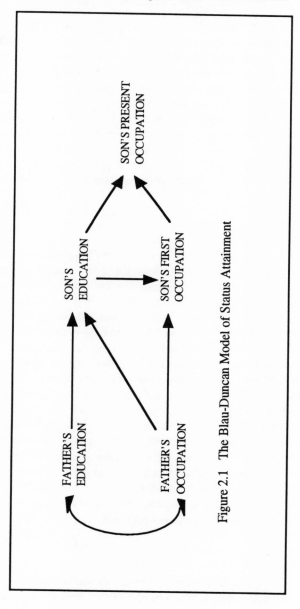

Figure 2.1   The Blau-Duncan Model of Status Attainment

supporting the hypothesis of the model (Kerckhoff and Huff 1974).

Nevertheless, the Blau-Duncan model estimation did not answer the following crucial questions (Haller and Portes 1973): (1) what are the mediating processes by which the father's social status exerts an influence on the son's educational and occupational attainment? And (2) in what specific ways are the son's mental (intellectual or cognitive) ability and academic performance related to his occupational status attainment? Answers to these questions required an examination of the causal process at more specific social-psychological levels. In this regard, "The Wisconsin model is the first major attempt to provide a social-psychological elaboration of the Blau-Duncan model" (Hawser, Tsai, and Sewell 1983, 20).

The Wisconsin Model

The Wisconsin model was similar to the Blau-Duncan model in the causal ordering of positional variables, even though it introduced a social-psychological orientation in the theoretical model. The Wisconsin model was first estimated by utilizing the data collected from American white men, who graduated from Wisconsin high schools in 1957, and were followed up in 1964. Among eight different variables (which are mental ability, parental socioeconomic status, academic performance, significant others' influence, the level of educational aspiration, the level of occupational aspiration, educational attainment, and occupational attainment), the causal relationships implied by the model were tested. In the Wisconsin model (see Figure 2.2), the straight solid lines stand for the causal paths of influence that are to be theoretically expected, the dotted lines stand for possibilities of theoretical relationships, and the curved line represents the unanalyzed correlation between variables that are not assigned causal priority.

Sewell, Haller, and Portes (1969) basically hypothesized as follows: Status attainment could be a strong combination of the function of (1) a cognitive-motivational component constructed by aspiration (ambition) and of (2) a contextual component constructed by social-psychological factors influencing their attainment. They further hypothesized that the effect of mental ability on the influence of significant others (such as parents, teachers, and friends) would be indirect through academic performance and that the effect of educational aspiration on occupational attainment would be indirect through educational attainment.

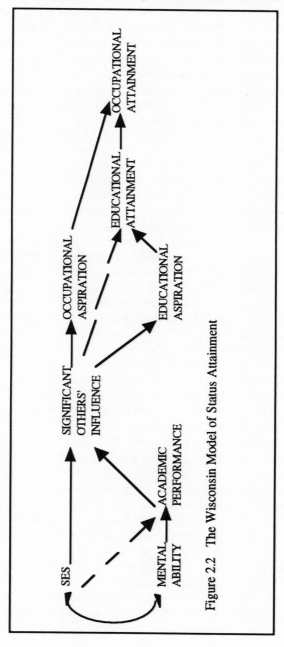

Figure 2.2 The Wisconsin Model of Status Attainment

In the Wisconsin model, educational aspiration and educational attainment were both measured as dichotomous variables: whether or not the male high school senior aspired to go to college, and whether or not the male actually obtained a bachelor's degree. Significant others' influence was measured by a summated score of four variables: whether or not the male high school senior was encouraged to go to college by (1) his father, (2) his mother, and (3) his teachers, in addition to (4) whether or not the male high school senior's close friends planned to go to college. The Wisconsin model estimation revealed, supporting the tentative hypothesis of the model, that significant others' influence (parents' influence, in particular) had an important direct effect (1) on educational and occupational aspirations and (2) on educational attainment. This estimation also revealed that significant others' influence was impacted directly by SES and indirectly by mental ability (hereinafter referred to as "ability") through academic performance. Each aspiration had a substantial influence on its respective attainment.

More important, the estimation of the Wisconsin model found that significant others' influence had a strong direct effect on the male high school senior's educational and occupational aspirations and on his educational and occupational attainment as well. This estimation also indicated the importance of the contribution of social-psychological influences in the development and the maintenance of status aspirations (Sewell and Hawser 1980). Presumably, students from high-SES families are more likely than students from low-SES families to score better on tests of cognitive skills because of their more favorable climates in developing cognitive abilities and because of their parents' emphasis placed on academic achievement.

The execution of enduring attitudes (such as educational and occupational aspirations), in Haller and Portes's (1973) words, could be a primary process in the early adult status attainment because such an execution not only represents a clear orientation toward aspirations but also involves a realistic assessment of chances conveyed to ego by significant others and one's own self-evaluations. Perhaps the estimation of the Wisconsin model has given evidence that the privileged effect of social origin on the subsequent attainment is significantly mediated especially by academic performance, social influence, and status aspiration in secondary education.

Early studies with the Wisconsin model only focused on the attainment process for white American men. The reason may lie in the fact that "The American dream [which is defined as American people want to be successful, and they want to live in a big house or make a lot of money] has been at the center of the nation's culture for centuries, yet until the 1960s it was [generally] reserved for white [men] only" (Feagin 1996, 429). In the 1960s, American women were part of the workforce; nevertheless, their occupational choices were limited to relatively few careers that were traditionally held by women, such as teaching, nursing, and secretarial work, even though they had graduated from college. More specifically, in general, women in those days did not have access to high-status occupations; at the same time, their social status was usually defined by their father's or husband's social standing. Many American women of that time (like many American women of today) also had the responsibility of fulfilling two roles: worker outside the home and worker inside the home.

Partial replications of the Wisconsin model for other samples of men (see, for example, Alexander, Eckland, and Griffin 1975; Crouse and Mueser 1978; Marini 1978; Porter 1974, 1976; Sewell and Hawser 1975; Wilson and Portes 1975) resulted in essentially the same conclusions as did Sewell, Haller, and Portes (1969) when reasonably comparable measures were used. Sewell (1971) further applied the original Wisconsin model to a sample of women who graduated from high school in 1957 (and followed up with a survey in 1975) and found that the process worked similarly for men and women. While the attainment process worked much the same for men and women, there were considerable differences between men and women in levels of educational and occupational aspirations and levels they actually attained. In order to enhance the advancement of women, the researchers concluded that women should have increased educational opportunities.

Women in American Higher Education

American higher education began in 1636 with the founding of Harvard College; nevertheless, it was not until 1837, when Oberlin College admitted four women, that American higher education became available for women: one of the major reasons for such a slow development of women's higher education was the idea that women could not physiologically stand the pressures of education (Feldman 1974). Further, educators feared that women would be corrupted by too much education and that education would make women seductive for evil (Tittle and Denker 1980). Such attitudes toward women continued in colonial America and finally began to change in the 1820s, not because of theological and cultural views but because of economic and political pressures of the times (Feldman 1974). Between 1860 and 1920, in effect, attending college became an accepted part of growing up for women in certain social groups, as it was for men (Solomon 1985).

The first significant advance in American graduate education began with the founding of three institutions: Clark University, Johns Hopkins University, and the University of Chicago (Spurr 1970). The University of Pennsylvania was the first one which declared in its 1885 catalog that "Women are admitted to any course for the doctoral degree under the same conditions as men" (Feldman 1974, 32), and when Columbia, Harvard, Yale, and Brown opened their graduate schools, those schools admitted women on the same criteria as men. Therefore, later decades of the 19th century and the early years of the 20th century are viewed as the beginning of a new era for American women with respect to opportunities in higher education.

The single most significant preoccupational variable determining occupational attainment for American men, as revealed by the Blau-Duncan and Wisconsin models, indeed, is educational attainment derived from educational opportunities. Over the past twenty years, American efforts for social reforms toward guaranteeing equal educational and occupational opportunities have undergone a considerable change by allowing women greater access to higher education (Ethington, Smart, and Pascarella 1991). The Equal Pay Act of 1963 was the initial landmark legislation barring discrimination at the federal level. The equal-pay-for-women legislation required that women be paid at the same wage rates as men if they were doing the same work (Congressional Quarterly Service 1965).

The above act was followed by Title VII of the Civil Rights Act of 1964 and Executive Order 11375 of 1967; both of which prohibited discrimination in employment particularly. Title IX of the Education Amendments of 1972 prohibited gender discrimination in federal educational programs. This legislation mandating equal opportunities for women was needed to overcome the segregation that had typified American educational (and occupational) stratification, inhibiting women's access to more prestigious and profitable occupations. Without the requisite educational attainment, women would still be denied entry into high status occupations dominantly held by men (Ethington et al. 1991).

During the first half of the 1970s, the percentage increase in college entrance for women did grow about twice as rapidly as the increase in college entrance for men (Blocher and Rapoza 1988). While the number of bachelor's and graduate degrees earned by women between the academic years of 1975-1976 and 1985-1986 rose 16 percent, men experienced a 6 percent decline in attaining those degrees (American Council on Education 1989). Unlike many other countries in the world, America has higher participation rates for women than for men in higher education; furthermore, women are more likely than men to complete bachelor's degrees (Bank 1995). Women comprise more than half of the degree recipients at all levels of American higher education of today, except for the doctoral level (Adelman 1992). Educational aspirations of American women have changed with dramatic increases in the number of women aspiring to graduate degrees, especially in the field of education (see. for example, Adelman 1992; Levine 1979; Roos and Jones 1993; Townsend and Mason 1990). In particular, the graduate school enrollment of women has been increasing faster than that of men in the United States (Syverson and Welch 1993).

Although the number of doctorates earned by women in the humanities and education has remained stable since 1984, according to Thurgood and Weinman (1991), the number of doctorates earned by women in life sciences and engineering has increased significantly since 1960. Women in life sciences earned 37 percent of all doctorates in 1990, albeit they outnumbered men in the subfield of health sciences in which they constituted 62 percent of the doctorates. This proportion has been the result of the number of women earning doctorates in nursing. In both social sciences and humanities, the gap between the numbers of men and women obtaining doctorates has narrowed considerably. While in 1960 women received only 13 percent of all social science doctorates and 16 percent of all humanities doctorates, they received 46 percent of the doctorates in each of those fields in 1990. Education was the only field in 1990 in which women were more numerous than men. It may be that academic careers (traditional university faculty positions) continue to be the major employment of new Ph.D. recipients in the labor force (Henschen 1993); however, it is also true that the proportion of new Ph.D.s moving into nonacademic employment has been growing over the past 20 years in the United

States (Greene 1995; Griffiths 1995).

Doctoral degrees earned by women may continue to account for an increasing share of all doctorates in the United States (Coll and Coll 1993; Leatherman 1995). The rising number of doctoral recipients, in fact, began in 1986; more specifically, while the number of doctorates awarded to women increased by more than 70 percent between the years 1975-1976 and 1990-1991, the number conferred on men dropped approximately 10 percent during the same period (Seltzer 1995). By the year 2001, the number of doctorates awarded to women is projected to surpass the number awarded to men (U.S. Department of Labor 1991). In summary, Title IX of the Education Amendments has served its purpose in opening educational (and eventually occupational) doors to American women.

Social Origin and Status Attainment

With women taking advantage of both educational and occupational opportunities provided to them, researchers began to focus on the status attainment of women. Among recent studies, Kalmijn (1994) and Lampard (1995) attempted to shed light on the relationship between social backgrounds and subsequent attainment levels. Kalmijn found that (1) the mother's occupation had a strong influence on the child's schooling career, and (2) the mother's occupation was as important for the son as for the daughter. Lampard found that both the mother's and the father's occupations had influences on the son's occupational attainment, while the latter was of markedly greater importance; in addition, the mother's occupation exerted a stronger influence on the daughter's occupational attainment than on the son's occupational attainment relative to the influence of the father's occupation. The findings of Kalmijn and Lampard supported the result obtained by Corcoran (1980) that the mother's occupation was more salient for the daughter's occupational attainment than for the son's occupational attainment. Anyway, the mother's occupational status appears to have an impact on the occupational and the income attainment of the child over and above the impact of the father's occupational status.

According to Updegraff (1996), however, it is the mother and the father together who are able to create an environment for facilitating the development and the maintenance of the child's educational and occupational aspirations. Updegraff has further argued that such an environment created by both parents does play an important role, especially in the daughter's intellectual development in her early adolescence. Aspiration, or ambition, is not necessarily a determinant of the future attainment but is potentially useful for the following major reasons (Gottfredson and Becker, cited in Rojewski 1996): (1) adolescents' aspirations tend to represent the orientation to their particular educational and occupational attainment; (2) adolescents' educational aspirations on occupational aspirations tend to have direct bearing on their eventual occupational attainment; and (3) adolescents' aspirations tend to play an active role in determining whether they pursue or ignore the educational opportunities available to them, especially in high school experiences.

Research on the process by which children or young people establish their educational and occupational aspirations has made the repeated use of the assumption that educational aspirations are most influenced by significant others, especially by parents (Kerckhoff and Huff, 1974). The intimate interaction between the parent and the child is the context within which the parental views of the child's future success are transmitted to the child. Using the data obtained from high school boys and their parents, Kerckhoff and Huff (1974) found that (1) the boy's report of the parents' aspirations reflected the boy's projection of his own aspirations, and (2) while the evidence of direct aspiration transmissions from the parents to the boy was stronger among the older boys, the parental influence in the form of the boy's modeling of the father was stronger among the younger boys.

Franklin (1995) revealed that (1) the students' socioeconomic backgrounds strongly influenced the "quality" of their efforts in academic pursuits and their perceptions of cognitive development and (2) the students' interactions with teachers and peers had a strong relationship with such academic pursuits and perceptions of cognitive development. However, motivations and attitudes may be indispensable no matter what the adolescents' future goals and plans are. That is, doing well in high school, like doing well in college, does lead the adolescent to widely increased opportunities in his or her adult and occupational world after all (Helen Dwight Reid Educational Foundation 1995).

In summary, educational qualifications appear to be the main path to status attainment. There is no doubt that an undergraduate degree (credential, to be exact) is a very real advantage in climbing the social ladder in American society. The focus in this study is therefore on the variables influencing (1) high school seniors' aspirations during the transition from high school to college and (2) their attainment levels in early adulthood. The next chapter describes the approach used to determine the economic, psychological, and social influences in educational attainment and early occupational attainment.

Chapter 3

Methodology

The first section of this chapter illustrates the path-analytic model proposed for this study. The second section provides the data and the sample for the proposed model. The third section describes the variables used as measures of the constructs of the proposed model. Finally, the last two sections are the descriptions of data analysis (namely path analysis as a research method) and of descriptive analysis.

The Path-Analytic Model

The factors influencing educational and occupational attainment were theorized in a longitudinal model incorporating the core constructs of the Wisconsin model based on the interaction of personal background variables (that is, social origin and social-psychological state) with subsequent educational and occupational aspirations and their attainment. Although each variable in the proposed model was hypothesized to influence both the educational and the occupational attainment variables, the manner in which the influence was exerted was expected to differ.

Figure 3.1 depicts the structure of the model, navigating the hypothesized process by which American women attain their social status. Each of the straight lines within the model indicates the hypothesized direct influence of one variable on another with the arrow indicating the direction of influence. The curved line indicates that two variables are related but no causal relationship is hypothesized between them. Particular interest in this study was determining if the attainment process for the sample of women was similar to the attainment process for the sample of men. A discussion of the theorized paths of influence in the model begins below.

The theoretical model for this study proposes that the respondent's academic performance is the very first endogenous variable and is dependent on the prior exogenous variables. Academic performance was hypothesized to be significantly determined by the respondent's personal background characteristics (SES) and the respondent's (cognitive) ability. Thus both SES and ability are exogenous variables; and, these two variables are determined by causes external to the model.

Both SES and academic performance were hypothesized to affect significant others' influence. "It is from this background that students begin their postsecondary education" (Ethington and Smart 1986, 289). In any event, research has continued to confirm that the influence of social origin is related to students' successes in higher education (Baird 1976). Baird further has contended that students from wealthier homes are more likely than students from poorer homes not only to attend graduate and professional schools but also to enter those schools immediately after college graduation. In the estimation of the Wisconsin model, both parental status and parental encouragement for male students to go to college had considerable influences on their obtaining an undergraduate degree.

The Wisconsin model has clarified the difference between students from wealthier homes and students from poorer homes in educational attainment which, in turn, could be the most reliable means to occupational attainment in American society. This difference may be sizable, no matter how educational attainment is defined, whether as a continuation in any kind of postsecondary education, college entry, and college graduation, as well as professional or graduate education.

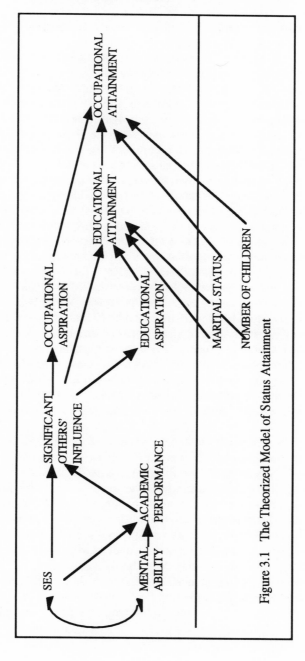

Figure 3.1   The Theorized Model of Status Attainment

It was further hypothesized that the dominant effect on educational and occupational aspirations would come from significant others' influence. Consistent with the Wisconsin theoretical model, no causal influence was anticipated between educational and occupational aspirations. In the model for this study, the effects of personal background characteristics (SES and ability) were expected to be manifested indirectly, mediated by both significant others' influence and academic performance. Consistent with the Wisconsin model, the determinants of educational attainment were hypothesized to be significant others' influence and educational aspiration.

At this point in the proposed model, additional sources of influence were added. Marriage (including spouses and children) influences are not considered to affect educational and occupational attainment for men but are considered to affect educational and occupational attainment for women (Airsman 1993). The attainment of women was hypothesized to be influenced by their marital status and the number of children they have. Yet, as Stoecker and Pascarella (1991) theorized, marital status and the number of children were both considered to be determined by factors outside the model as control variables. While these variables were presumed to be caused by external factors, they did not fit as exogenous variables, since the placement of variables within the model presumed a temporal sequence. Endogenous variables are considered to have explicit causes within the model, and these variables were not presumed to be caused by any endogenous variable inside the model. These variables were of research interest and were tested to determine what their effects were, if any, on educational and occupational attainment.

Although significant direct effects were not expected from SES, the continuing influence of SES was anticipated to be evidenced by a strong positive, indirect effect. The final variable in the path-analytic model was occupational attainment, which was hypothesized to be dominantly determined by occupational aspiration, educational attainment, marital status, and the number of children. All influences within the model were hypothesized to be positive, but no direction of influence was hypothesized for marital status and the number of children.

Readers, who are familiar with the research literature of higher education, may at first glance consider the model for this study to be misspecified by the omission of the traditional measures of institutional characteristics and student involvement within postsecondary *schools can have lasting effects*

institutions. In effect, educational research has continued to examine school determinants of student achievement or degree persistence in secondary and postsecondary education (see, for example, Biniaminov and Glasman 1983; Cabrera, Nora, and Castaneda 1993; Duran and Weffer 1992; Ethington 1992; Franklin 1995; Hearn 1987; Lamport 1993; Page and Keith 1981; Pascarella and Terenzini 1980; Sander and Krautmann 1995; Smart 1986; Smith, Morrison, and Wolf, 1994; Terenzini and Pascarella 1978; Tinto 1975; Townsend and Mason 1990; Zweigenhaft 1993). At the same time, educational research has continued to compare the effects of women's colleges and coeducational colleges on the occupational and economic attainment of women (see, for example, Astin 1993; Carrigan 1995; Kim 1995; Ledman 1995; Reeves 1994; Riordan 1994; Rothstein 1995; Smith, Wolf, and Morrison 1995; Stoecker and Pascarella 1991; Tidball 1985, 1986).

The theoretical model for this study was not a college-effects study focusing only on women who had pursued a postsecondary education following high school graduation. In order for the attainment process for women to be fully understood, it was imperative that the sample of Americans includes those who had reached all levels of educational attainment. This was particularly important in examining the sample for this study because only 58 percent of the study sample obtained a bachelor's degree or higher. The majority of research efforts (including the aforementioned studies) on the status attainment of American women have focused only on women who had attended college, yielding information more on institutional effects on those women's attainment levels rather than on their attainment processes.

Data and Sample

The study sample was drawn from the data of the National Longitudinal Study of the High School Class of 1972 (NLS-72), sponsored by the National Center for Educational Statistics (NCES) with support from various elements of the U.S. Office of Education that had special interests in the long-range effects of educational policy. According to the NCES (1976), the main goal of the NLS-72 was to furnish a factual basis for verifying and refining federal policy concerned with maximizing individual access to educational and occupational opportunities and aiding young people to assume a productive adult role in society. The sample design for the NLS-72 is a deeply stratified two-stage probability sample with schools as first-stage sampling units and students as second-stage units. In the first stage, a stratified probability sample of 1,200 schools was selected; then in the second stage, a simple random sample of 18 seniors per school was chosen (NCES 1977). Accordingly, the population consisted of all 12th-graders enrolled during 1972 in public and private high schools in the 50 states and the District of Columbia. The first-stage sampling frame was constructed from computerized school files, which were maintained by the Office of Education and by the National Catholic Educational Association (NCES 1975).

The NLS-72 was particularly designed to provide information on the educational and occupational development of adolescents during their transition from high school to the adult and occupational world. The NLS-72 data were composed of a broad array of information on personal backgrounds, academic performance, attitudes, values, educational and occupational aspirations, and educational and occupational attainment. The NLS-72 first surveyed the national sample of high school seniors in the spring of 1972 and followed up in the fall of 1973, 1974, 1976, 1979, and 1986, respectively. Response rates across the first five individual surveys exceeded 90 percent, and they exceeded 88 percent on the fifth follow-up survey in 1986 (NCES 1988).

The NLS-72 data were particularly appropriate in addressing the research questions posed in this study because the initiation of the NLS-72 was the year in which Title IX of the Education Amendments was enacted. The NLS-72 provided information on the activities and attitudes of respondents (approximately 18 years old) in 1972, the consequences of their alternative choices and experiences from 1972 to 1986, and outcomes from such choices and experiences during their early thirties in 1986. What made the data especially attractive was that they followed the survey participants for 14 years after high school graduation, facilitating an examination of the labor-market experience and educational attainment. The study reported here was based on the data from the respondents who had complete data on all the variables described in the next section.

Variables

The model estimated in this study included ten different variables (as illustrated in Figure 3.1), which were ordered in a causal sequence. While seven variables were measured as single items, three variables were measured as four-item scales. SES was a composite of four items: the family income, the father's and the mother's education, and the family occupational status. Occupations of the father and the mother, along with the family income, were taken from the 1972 base-year survey. Because of extensive missing data on the 1972 survey that provided a measure of the father's and the mother's education, the NLS composite indicator of the father's and the mother's education was used.

By the same token, because of extensive missing data on the father's and the mother's occupations, a single variable indicating the family occupational status was created: that is, if the father's occupational status was higher than the mother's occupational status, then the father's occupational status was used as the indicator of the family occupational status; if the mother's occupational status was higher than the father's, the mother's was used; if the mother's occupation was missing, the father's was used; and if the father's occupation was missing, the mother's was used.

After coding each of the father's and the mother's occupations to Duncan's (1961) socioeconomic index (SEI)[1] classification system, a principal-components analysis was conducted to determine whether or not the four variables (that is, the father's education, the mother's education, the family income, and the family occupational status) were unidimensional, warranting a single measure of socioeconomic status. One factor was extracted, with the factor loadings of each variable essentially the same (see Table 3.1 for the results of the principal-components analysis). The single measure of socioeconomic status was then constructed by summing after standardizing the education of (1) the father and (2) the mother, (3) the family income, and (4) the family occupational status. Finally, the internal consistency reliability of the four-item scale was .795.

Ability was operationalized using the formula score[2] from the 1972 base-year test battery in four areas: vocabulary (the ability to understand the English language), reading (the ability to read and to understand short passages of nontechnical materials), letter groups (the ability to find general concepts in a nonverbal context), and mathematics (the ability to solve reasoning problems involving quantitative comparisons, yet not requiring algebraic, geometric, or trigonometric skills). This test battery was developed by the Educational Testing Service (ETS) in New Jersey to measure both verbal and nonverbal ability (for the details of these four types of tests, see Appendix A). A principal-components analysis was conducted to determine whether or not the four test scores were unidimensional, warranting a single measure of ability, and one factor was extracted, with the factor loadings of each variable essentially the same (see Table 3.1 for the results of the principal-components analysis). The single measure of ability was constructed by summing after standardizing the scores in (1) vocabulary, (2) reading, (3) letter groups, and (4) mathematics. The internal consistency reliability of the four-item scale was .798.

Table 3.1   Results of Principal-Components Analysis

Item	Factor Coefficient
Parental Socioeconomic Status:	
Father's Educational Level	.83303
Family Occupational Status	.81671
Family Income	.75950
Mother's Educational Level	.73832
Mental Ability:	
Reading	.82736
Mathematics	.81378
Vocabulary	.76984
Letter Groups	.74555

Significant others' influence taken from the 1972 base-year survey was measured as a composite of four items: (1) the father's, (2) the mother's, and (3) the teachers' encouragement for the respondent to go to college, in addition to (4) the respondent's close friends' plans to go to college. The encouragement of each of the father's and the mother's was constructed from the items reflecting the educational levels desired for the respondent with six response categories ranging from less than high school graduation to graduate or professional school attainment. They were recoded such that 1 = no college and 2 = college. Teachers' encouragement was constructed from the item reflecting encouragement for the respondent to go to college, with the following three response categories: discouraged, did not try to influence, and encouraged. It was recoded such that 1 = did not encourage and 2 = encouraged. The plan of friends was constructed from the item reflecting educational plans soon after the high school graduation with six response categories: military service, vocational school, full-time homemaker, college, on-the-job training, and full-time worker. It was recoded such that 1 = will not go to college and 2 = will go to college. The measure of significant others' influence was constructed by summing across the father's, the mother's, and the teachers' encouragement for college education, along with the friends' plans. The internal consistency reliability of the four-item scale was .603.

Academic performance (actual percentile rank in high school class), educational aspiration (coded: 1 = less than high school, 2 = high school, 3 = vocational school, 4 = two-year college, 5 = four-year college, and 6 = graduate or professional school), and occupational aspiration (the respondent's aspired occupational status coded to Duncan's SEI classification system) were all taken from the 1972 base-year survey. Educational attainment (coded: 1 = some high school, 2 = high school diploma, 3 = vocational school, 4 = some college, 5 = college graduation, 6 = master's degree, and 7 = doctoral or professional degree) and occupational attainment (the respondent's attained occupational status coded to Duncan's SEI classification system) were both taken from the 1986 fifth follow-up survey.

Finally, the two control variables (marital status and the number of children) were taken from the 1986 fifth follow-up survey. As stated before, SES and ability were considered to be exogenous variables determined by factors outside the causal system of the model. With the exceptions of marital status and the number of children (which were included as both control and research interest variables for the status attainment process for women), all other variables were considered to be endogenous variables determined within the causal system of the model.

Table 3.2 presents full operational definitions of all the variables for this study, and Table 3.3 shows a comparison of the variables used in both the Wisconsin model and the current model.

Table 3.2   Operational Definitions of Variables

Variables	Definitions
Exogenous Variables: Socioeconomic Status (1972)	A four-item scale based on the educational level of (1) the father and (2) the mother, (3) the family occupational status, and (4) the family income, with five levels (from "less than high school diploma" to "graduate degree"). Duncan's (1961) socioeconomic index (SEI) classification system was used for family occupational status and 10 income levels (from "less than 3,000" to more than"18,000"). All items were standardized and summed. Internal consistency reliability = .795.
Ability (1972)	A four-item scale based on test scores of the respondent in four areas: (1) vocabulary, (2) reading, (3) letter groups, and (4) mathematics. All items were standardized and summed. Internal consistency reliability = .798.
Endogenous Variables: Academic Performance (1972)	A single item assessing the respondent's rank in the high school class. The rank was measured as the actual percentile rank.
Significant Others' Influence (1972)	A four-item scale based on the respondent's report of significant others' influence: whether or not (1) the father, (2) the mother, and (3) the teachers encouraged the respondent to go to college, and (4) whether or not the respondent's close friends planned to go to college. All items were summed. Internal consistency reliability = .603.

Table 3.2 (Continued)

Variables	Definitions
Educational Aspiration (1972)	A single item measuring the respondent's educational aspiration level with six categories ranging from "less than high school" to "graduate or professional school."
Occupational Aspiration (1972) *drops*	A single item measuring the level of occupational status to which the respondent aspired. Each of the aspired occupations was coded using Duncan's (1961) SEI classification system.
Educational Attainment (1986)	A single item measuring the highest degree earned by the respondent in 1986 with seven response categories form "some high school" to "doctoral or professional degree."
Occupational Attainment (1986) *drops of who aren't working?*	A single item measuring the level of occupational status to which the respondent attained in 1986. Each of the attained occupations was coded using Duncan's SEI classification system.
Control Variables: Marital Status (1986)	A single item reflecting whether the respondent had married or had marriage-like relationships. (Originally coded: 1 = yes, 2 = no; then recoded 1 = no, 2 = yes).
Number of Children (1986)	A single item measuring the number of children the respondent had with five response categories (from "none" to "seven or more").

Table 3.3   Measures in the Wisconsin and Current Models

Wisconsin Model	Current Model
1. Mental Ability: Henmon-Nelson test score.	1. Mental ability: Verbal and nonverbal tests by ETS.
2. SES: A composite of the father's and mother's education, father's occupation, and family income.	2. SES: A composite of the father's and mother's education, father's occupation, and family income.
3. Academic Performance*: The respondent's high school rank.	3. Academic Performance*: The respondent's high school rank.
4. Significant Other's Influence*: The parents' and teachers' encouragement for college; and friends' plan for college.	4. Significant Other's Influence*: The parents' and teachers' encouragement for college; and friends' plan for college.
5. Educational Aspiration: Whether or not the respondent aspired to go to college.	5. Educational Aspiration: The respondent's aspired highest level of education.
6. Occupational Aspiration*: Duncan's SEI scores of occupational status aspired by the respondent.	6. Occupational Aspiration*: Duncan's SEI scores of occupational status aspired by the respondent.
	7. Marital Status: The respondent had married or married-like relationships.
	8. Number of Children: The number of children the respondent had.
7. Educational Attainment: Whether or not the respondent obtained a bachelor's degree.	9. Educational Attainment: The highest degree the respondent attained in 1986.
8. Occupational Attainment*: Duncan's SEI scores of Occupational status attained by the respondent.	10. Occupational Attainment*: Duncan's SEI scores of Occupational status attained by the respondent.

*Four common measures were used in both studies.

Path Analysis

In this study path analysis was used to estimate the influences on status attainment. Path analysis (developed by Sewell Wright in the 1920s) has been embraced as an appropriate, powerful, and theory-driven approach to the analysis of nonexperimental data (Keith 1988). In short, path analysis is a research method for presenting a causal model in which a series of independent variables is used to predict a series of dependent variables. At its simplest level, path analysis uses multiple regression analysis but in a structured and explicit manner (Keith 1988).

An intriguing aspect of path analysis, according to Sobel (1982, 291), is that "It makes explicit the direct and indirect effects of causal variables on dependent variables and thereby allows for a detailed substantive accounting of the sociological process under investigation." The primary purpose of path analysis is to separate the correlations among variables into causal and noncausal components based on the theory of cause and effect: indeed, according to Keith, Harrison, and Ehly (1987, 208), "It is this specification of an explicit theory that is at the heart of path analysis, and the theory is displayed in a path model."

Path analysis, which has its roots in economics and sociology in which true experimental studies are rare, is now prevalent in psychological and educational research. Although many people have contributed to the introduction of path analysis to social and behavioral sciences, the 1967 Blau-Duncan model is of primary importance because it built a framework for examining occupational mobility (Wolfle 1985). Emphasizing that the unsolved path model is a visual representation of the theory of cause and effect, Keith (1988) has stated that it is this explicit, visual statement of theory that is at the heart of path analysis and is the most important step in the path-analytic model. Keith has further maintained that if a researcher accepts the theory, and the data are adequate, then the researcher must accept the results of path analysis (that is, the numbers generated are the implications of the data and theory in combination).

Although path analysis encourages researchers to consider all important potential causes of the dependent measure within a theory-based context, like any nonexperimental research, the primary danger in path analysis is causality. According to Keith (1988), the main three logical requirements for inferring causality of this type are: (1) prior time precedence must be established (that is, the presumed cause must happen before the presumed effect); (2) there must be a relationship between the variables (a condition satisfied by a correlation between variables); and (3) such a relationship must be nonspurious.

Prior to estimating the theoretical model for this study, a preliminary analysis was conducted to determine whether or not the influence of the variables differed for men and women. Otherwise, if the results of the estimation of the model for this study were found to differ from those reported by Sewell, Haller, and Portes (1969), it might have been (1) because the samples of the two models came from different samples or (2) because the measure for educational attainment was different between them. A dichotomous variable (whether or not the respondent obtained an undergraduate degree) was used in the Wisconsin model, whereas a continuous variable (the highest academic degree the respondent obtained) was used in this study.

In order to determine if the influence within the model was the same for men and women, the interaction terms between the variable indicating "sex" (1 = male, 2 = female) and other independent variables in the model were computed. For each equation defining the model, the appropriate interaction terms were added; then the increase in the amount of variance explained was tested for significance (see Table 3.4 for the results of the interaction tests). For each equation the change in R-squared was significant ($p < .001$). However, none of the increments in variance explained (all approximately 1 percent or less) were considered substantively important; and, the levels of significance were considered to be the result of the large sample size.

The effects of the variables within the model were then considered to be the same for both genders. More specifically, the attainment process is the same, yet sex can still play a role in the model because men and women may differ in constructs, but the relationships among the constructs are similar for both sexes. The model for this study was then estimated for the combined sample of men and women ($N = 2,160$); the variable sex was included as an exogenous variable in the path-analytic model for this study.

Table 3.4   Interactions of Sex with Other Independent Variables

Dependent Variables	R^2	R^2-Change	p
Equation 1 (Academic Performance):			
Without Interaction Terms	.32962	.0000	
With Interaction Terms	.33251	.00289*	.0000
Equation 2 (Significant Others' Influence):			
Without Interaction Terms	.07588	.0000	
With Interaction Terms	.08684	.01096*	.0000
Equation 3 (Educational Aspiration):			
Without Interaction Terms	.28039	.0000	
With Interaction Terms	.28579	.00539*	.0000
Equation 4 (Occupational Aspiration):			
Without Interaction Terms	.15098	.0000	
With Interaction Terms	.16084	.00986*	.0000
Equation 5 (Educational Attainment):			
Without Interaction Terms	.36195	.0000	
With Interaction Terms	.36579	.00384*	.0000
Equation 6 (Occupational Attainment):			
Without Interaction Terms	.26365	.0000	
With Interaction Terms	.27534	.01169*	.0000

Descriptive Analysis

Exploratory Analysis

Data were checked for the assumptions underlying the application of multiple regression: normality and homoscedasticity. The close examination of the NLS-72 data revealed no substantial deviation from normality and homoscedasticity. The normal probability plot was linear and residuals plots appeared random. In addition, no multicollinearity was present, for all the variance inflation factors for each of the six equations were less than 1.5.

The GEMINI Program

The direct and indirect effects implied by the proposed model were estimated from means, standard deviations, and correlations (see Table 3.5) among all the variables used as input into Wolfle and Ethington's (1985) GEMINI program based on Sobel's (1982) work. Ordinary least-squares procedures were used to estimate the coefficients of each of the equations defining the model with each endogenous variable regressed on all exogenous variables and causally antecedent endogenous variables. The GEMINI program written in FORTRAN, produces the indirect effects and their standard errors, along with usual regression results.

All the possible causal paths of influence in the model were estimated to test whether the paths hypothesized to be zero were nonsignificant. The direct effects are represented by regression coefficients, either standardized (beta weights) or unstandardized (*b* weights), which were interpreted in the usual manner. The indirect effects are estimated by the sums of the products of the direct effects through intervening variables in the model. Specifically, the indirect effects indicate the influence on the dependent variable that is the result of directly influencing the prior causal variables in the model. Comparisons of the relative influence of variables within an equation are made by examining the standardized coefficients. Consistent with the recommendation of Land (1969) and Pedhazur (1982), only standardized effects greater than .05 are considered of substantial importance in this study.

Table 3.5 Correlations, Means, and Standard Deviations for Variables in the Model of Status Attainment

	1	2	3	4	5	6	7	8	9	10	11
1. SES	1										
2. Sex	-.027	1									
3. Ability	.320	-.029	1								
4. Academic Performance	.084	.202	.525	1							
5. Sig. Others' Influence	.130	.025	.228	.235	1						
6. Edu. Aspiration	.302	-.126	.375	.289	.359	1					
7. Occ. Aspiration	.190	-.195	.257	.241	.116	.380	1				
8. Marital Status	-.054	.016	-.027	-.008	-.054	-.095	-.043	1			
9. Number of Children	-.127	.086	-.100	-.053	-.047	-.126	-.121	.431	1		
10. Edu. Attainment	.285	-.109	.406	.371	.247	.482	.359	-.103	-.193	1	
11. Occ. Attainment	.192	-.068	.257	.249	.088	.245	.321	-.057	-.144	.476	1
Mean	.016	1.520	.030	68.840	6.771	5.280	64.044	1.848	1.178	4.788	58.416
Standard Deviation	3.151	.500	3.140	24.387	1.202	.991	19.270	.359	1.118	1.050	19.670

Final Sample

Respondents with missing values (or out-of-range values) on any of the variables in the proposed model were necessarily excluded from the final sample for this study. A large sample is desirable when estimating path models using the GEMINI program (Wolfle and Ethington 1985). Of the 22,652 individuals originally participating in the 1972 base-year survey, nevertheless, only 12,841 participated in the 1986 fifth follow-up survey, losing 9,811 respondents. Table 3.6 explains the loss of the participants on the successive variables used in the model. There were extensive missing data on such measures as the family occupational status, the family income, the father's encouragement, the educational aspiration, the teachers' encouragement, the educational attainment, and the occupational aspiration. The sample used for the path analysis reported here consisted of only 2,160 respondents who had complete data on all the variables used in the model for this study.

Mean Comparisons

Because such a large proportion of the NLS original sample was lost due to the missing data, mean comparisons were made between the NLS full and final samples on variables used in the model for this study. Table 3.7 presents the mean and the standard deviation on each measure for both samples; and the sample size on each measure for the full sample is given. The final sample obviously differs from the full sample. In particular, the final sample of Americans, who came from higher socioeconomic families (based on the mother's and the father's education, the father's and the mother's occupations, and the family income), had higher levels of ability (except for reading), educational and occupational aspirations, as well as educational and occupational attainment.

Based on the sample selection criteria and the procedure of data analysis for the causal model described in this chapter, the final sample for this study was evidently not representative of the general population of the National Longitudinal Study of the High School Class of 1972 (NLS-72). Accordingly, no attempt was made to generalize to the NLS full population and, therefore, the results of the estimation of the model for this study was considered unique to the sample of this study.

Table 3.6　The Loss of Participants in Successive Variables[a]

22,652 - 9,811 (nonparticipant in the 1986 survey)　　　$N = 12,841$

1	Lost	(0)	on sex	$N = 12,841$
2	Lost	(3,943)	on family occupational status	$N = 8,898$
3	Lost	(58)	on father's education	$N = 8,840$
4	Lost	(15)	on mother's education	$N = 8,825$
5	Lost	(1,646)	on family income	$N = 7,179$
6	Lost	(310)	on test score in vocabulary	$N = 6,869$
7	Lost	(0)	on test score in reading	$N = 6,869$
8	Lost	(0)	on test score in letter groups	$N = 6,869$
9	Lost	(0)	on test score in mathematics	$N = 6,869$
10	Lost	(482)	on academic performance	$N = 6,387$
11	Lost	(729)	on teachers' encouragement	$N = 5,658$
12	Lost	(91)	on friends' college plans	$N = 5,567$
13	Lost	(934)	on father's encouragement	$N = 4,633$
14	Lost	(217)	on mother's encouragement	$N = 4,416$
15	Lost	(905)	on educational aspiration	$N = 3,511$
16	Lost	(581)	on occupational aspiration	$N = 2,930$
17	Lost	(12)	on marital status	$N = 2,918$
18	Lost	(11)	on the number of children	$N = 2,907$
19	Lost	(665)	on educational attainment	$N = 2,242$
20	Lost	(82)	on occupational attainment	$N = 2,160$

Therefore, the final sample　　　$N = 2,160$

[a]The last column represents the resulting sample size after the deletion of respondents with missing data on the row variable.

Table 3.7   Means of the NLS Full and Final Samples[a]

	Variable	Full Sample Mean	Final Sample Mean
1.	Sex	1.521(.500) ($N = 14,479$)	1.520(.500) ($N = 2,160$)
2.	Parental Socioeconomic Status (SES):		
	Father's education	2.316(1.273) ($N = 14,169$)	2.723(1.324) ($N = 2,160$)
	Mother's education	2.175(1.058) ($N = 14,222$)	2.493(1.098) ($N = 2,160$)
	Father's occupation	42.287(24.748) ($N = 14,116$)	49.654(25.078) ($N = 2,160$)
	Mother's occupation	41.829(21.091) ($N = 7,482$)	47.797(19.844) ($N = 2,160$)
	Parental income	5.553(2.925) ($N = 16,575$)	6.634(2.711) ($N = 2,160$)
3.	Ability:		
	Vocabulary	6.016(4.158) ($N = 15,860$)	8.400(3.886) ($N = 2,160$)
	Reading	15.794(6.015) ($N = 15,860$)	12.430(4.178) ($N = 2,160$)
	Letter groups	9.321(5.116) ($N = 15,860$)	19.081(4.127) ($N = 2,160$)
	Mathematics	12.254(7.426) ($N = 15,860$)	17.318(5.972) ($N = 2,160$)
4.	Academic Performance	52.545(28.025) ($N = 16,905$)	68.840(24.387) ($N = 2,160$)

[a]Standard deviations are given in the first parentheses, and the sample sizes are given in the second parentheses.

Table 3.7 (Continued)

Variable	Full Sample Mean	Final Sample Mean
5. Significant Others' Influence:		
Father's encouragement	1.417(.493) (*N* = 16,142)	1.572(.495) (*N* = 2,160)
Mother's encouragement	1.414(.493) (*N* = 17,213)	1.572(.495) (*N* = 2,160)
Teachers' encouragement	1.657(.475) (*N* = 16,505)	1.788(.409) (*N* = 2,160)
Friends' college plans	2.419(1.977) (*N* = 20,441)	1.839(.367) (*N* = 2,160)
6. Educational Aspiration	4.687(1.327) (*N* = 11,172)	5.280(.991) (*N* = 2,160)
7. Occupational Aspiration	54.957(22.129) (*N* = 12,915)	64.044(19.270) (*N* = 2,160)
8. Marital Status	1.861(.346) (*N* = 12,761)	1.848(.359) (*N* = 2,160)
9. Number of Children	1.376(1.151) (*N* = 12,707)	1.178(1.118) (*N* = 2,160)
10. Educational Attainment	4.533(1.107) (*N* = 8,439)	4.788(1.050) (*N* = 2,160)
11. Occupational Attainment	51.153(21.802) (*N* = 11,473)	58.416(19.670) (*N* = 2,160)

[a]Standard deviations are given in the first parentheses, and the sample sizes are given in the second parentheses.

Notes

1. Duncan (1961) created a socioeconomic index (SEI) of occupational status by ranking occupation groups on the basis of their differences in education and income (Blau 1975).

2. Computation for formula scores (FS) in the test battery was FS = R - [W/(C - 1)]; where R = number of right responses; W = number of wrong responses; C = number of item response alternatives (NCES 1981).

Chapter 4

Results

This chapter details the results of the model estimation of this study. The direct effects in the model are given in Table 4.1. The indirect effects are given in Table 4.2. The direct effects, the indirect effects, and the total effects, as well as the dominant mediators of the indirect effects on educational and occupational attainment are summarized in Tables 4.3 and 4.4. To visualize the causal paths of influence in the model, Figure 4.1 diagrams all the significant direct effects that were listed in Table 4.1. The details of the estimation of the model begin below.

Direct Effects

The estimated coefficients of each of the six equations defining the model are indicated in both standardized (beta weights) and unstandardized (*b* weights) forms (see Table 4.1). The coefficients are direct paths and represent the direct effects of the individual predictor variables on the respective dependent variables. Each coefficient

Table 4.1　Direct Effects in the Status Attainment Process[a]

| | 4 acad perform | 5 sig others inf | Dependent Variables | | | |
			6 educ aspir	7 OCC aspir	10 ed attain	11 OCC attain
1.SES	-.089**	079**	.197**	.135**	.107**	.048
	(-.691)	(.030)	(.062)	(.823)	(.036)	(.298)
2.Sex	.216**	-.004	-.154**	-.236**	-.077**	-.005
	(10.527)	(-.009)	(-.304)	(-9.089)	(-.161)	(-.214)
3.Ability	.560**	.114**	.166**	.080*	.116**	.026
	(4.348)	(.043)	(.053)	(.492)	(.039)	(.163)
4.Academic Performance		.170**	.154**	.228**	.193**	.068*
		(.008)	(.006)	(.180)	(.008)	(.055)
5.Significant Others' Influence			.263**	.033	.049*	-.043
			(.217)	(.523)	(.043)	(-.700)
6.Educational Aspiration					.260**	-.038
					(.275)	(-.760)
7.Occupational Aspiration					.131**	.163**
					(.007)	(.166)
8.Marital Status					-.019	.008
					(-.055)	(.451)
9.Number of Children					-.092**	-.047
					(-.086)	(-.827)
10.Educational Attainment						.388**
						(7.278)
11.Occupational Attainment						
R-squared	.330	.076	.280	.151	.362	.263

(handwritten: 2 = female, 1 = male)

[a]Unstandardized (metric) coefficients are given in parentheses.
*p < .01; **p < .001.

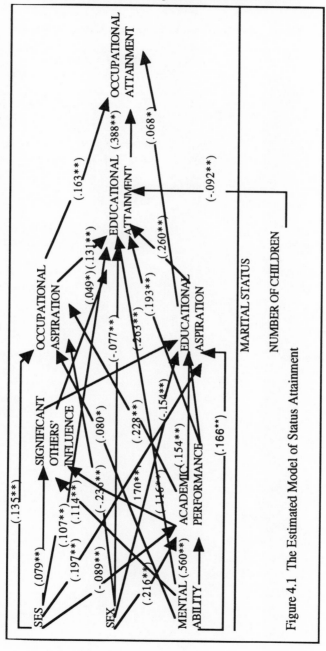

Figure 4.1 The Estimated Model of Status Attainment

Table 4.2 Indirect Effects in the Status Attainment Process[a]

		Dependent Variables				
	4	5	6	7	10	11
1. SES	-	-.015**	.003	-.018**	.053**	.065**
	-	(-.006)	(.001)	(-.112)	(.018)	(.404)
2. Sex	-	.037**	.042**	.050**	-.010	-.046**
	-	(.088)	(.083)	(1.934)	(-.021)	(-1.821)
3. Ability	-	.095**	.141**	.134**	.227**	.185**
	-	(.036)	(.045)	(.824)	(.076)	(1.160)
4. Academic Performance	-	.045**	.006	.091**	.133**	
	-	(.002)	(.004)	(.004)	(.108)	
5. Significant Others' Influence			-	-	.073**	.043**
			-	-	(.063)	(.697)
6. Educational Aspiration					-	.101**
					-	(2.003)
7. Occupational Aspiration					-	.051**
					-	(.052)
8. Marital Status					-	-.007
					-	(-.398)
9. Number of Children					-	-.036**
					-	(-.629)
10. Educational Attainment					-	-
					-	-
11. Occupational Attainment						

[a]Unstandardized coefficients are given in parentheses.

*p < .01; **p < .001.

indicates the average amount of change in the dependent variable produced by a unit change in the independent variable when the other independent variables in the equation are held constant.

Academic Performance

The three prior variables (SES, sex, and ability) in the model explained 33 percent (R-squared = .330) of the variance in academic performance (high school rank). The theoretical model of the study posited that dominant effects on academic performance should come from SES and ability. All the three variables had significant direct effects in the following order of magnitude: ability (beta = .560), sex (beta = .216), and SES (beta = -.089). The negative coefficient for SES indicates that students from low-SES backgrounds demonstrate higher academic performance, while the reverse is true for students from high-SES backgrounds. The positive effect of ability indicates that students of higher ability are more likely than students of lower ability to demonstrate higher academic performance. The positive effect of sex indicates that women are more likely than men to demonstrate higher academic performance. Anyway, ability has by far the strongest effect on academic performance.

Significant Others' Influence

The four prior variables (SES, sex, ability, and academic performance) in the model explained 7.6 percent (R-squared = .076) of the variance in significant others' influence. The theoretical model posited that dominant effects on significant others' influences should come from SES and academic performance. Three of the four variables had significant direct positive influences in the following order of magnitude: academic performance (beta = .170), ability (beta = .114), and SES (beta = .079). The positive effects of the three variables indicate that the higher the SES, ability, and academic performance are, the higher the significant others' influence will be.

Educational Aspiration

The five prior variables (SES, sex, ability, academic performance, and significant others' influence) in the model explained 28 percent (R-squared = .280) of the variance in educational aspiration. The theoretical model posited that the dominant influence on educational aspiration should come from significant others' influence. Each of the five variables had a significant direct effect in the following order of magnitude: significant others' influence (beta = .263), SES (beta = .197), ability (beta = .166), academic performance (beta = .154), and sex (beta = -.154). The negative coefficient for sex indicates that men are more likely than women to aspire to higher levels of educational attainment. The positive effects of the other four variables indicate that the higher the SES, ability, academic performance, and significant others' influence are, the higher the educational aspiration levels will be.

Occupational Aspiration

The five prior variables (SES, sex, ability, academic performance, and significant others' influence) in the model explained 15.1 percent (R-squared = .151) of the variance in occupational aspiration. The theoretical model posited that the dominant influence on occupational aspiration should come from significant others' influence; contrary to this hypothesis, the effect of significant others' influence was indeed nonsignificant for this sample. Yet the four remaining variables had significant direct effects in the following order of magnitude: sex (beta = -.236), academic performance (beta = .228), SES (beta = .135), and ability (beta = .080). The negative coefficient for sex indicates that men are more likely than women to aspire to higher status occupations. The positive effects of the other three variables indicate that the higher the SES, ability, and academic performance are, the higher the occupational aspiration will be.

Educational Attainment

The seven prior variables (SES, sex, ability, academic performance, significant others' influence, educational aspiration, and occupational aspiration), along with the two control variables (marital status and the number of children), in the model explained 36.2 percent (R-squared = .362) of the variance in educational attainment. The theoretical model posited that dominant influences on educational attainment should come from educational aspiration, significant others' influence, marital status, and the number of children. Eight of the nine variables had direct effects in the following order of magnitude: educational aspiration (beta = .260), academic performance (beta = .193), occupational aspiration (beta = .131), ability (beta = .116); SES (beta = .107); children (beta = -.092); sex (beta = -.077), and significant others' influence (beta = .049). The negative coefficient for the number of children indicates that those who have fewer children are more likely than those who have more children to attain higher levels of education. The negative coefficient for sex indicates that men are more likely than women to attain higher levels of education. The positive effects of the other six variables indicate that the higher the SES, ability, academic performance, significant others' influence, educational aspiration, and occupational aspiration are, the higher the educational attainment will be.

Occupational Attainment

The eight prior variables (SES, sex, ability, academic performance, significant others' influence, educational aspiration, occupational aspiration, and educational attainment), along with the two control variables (marital status and the number of children), in the model explained 26.3 percent (R-squared = .263) of the variance in occupational attainment. The theoretical model posited that dominant influences on occupational attainment should come from occupational aspiration, educational attainment, marital status, and children.

Three of the ten variables had direct effects in the following order of magnitude: educational attainment (beta = .388), occupational aspiration (beta = .163), and academic performance (beta = .068). The positive effects of these variables indicate that the higher the academic performance, occupational aspiration, and educational attainment are, the higher the occupational attainment will be.

Indirect and Total Effects

The indirect effects are estimated by the sum of the products of the direct effects through mediating variables in the model. The total effects are the sum of the direct and indirect effects in each equation for the respective variables in the model. All of the indirect effects within the model are given in Table 4.2. With the exception of ability, the indirect effects of the variables in the model were relatively small, albeit many of them reached a level of statistical significance. Since the primary focus of this study is on educational and occupational attainment, only the indirect and total effects on these attainment variables are described. Tables 4.3 and 4.4 present the direct, indirect, and the total effects, along with the mediating variables for the indirect effects, on educational and occupational attainment.

Educational Attainment

Four variables were found to have significant indirect effects on educational attainment in the following order of magnitude (see Table 4.3): ability, academic performance, significant others' influence, and SES. The strongest indirect effect on educational attainment came from ability. The effect of ability was much stronger than those of others. SES had a positive indirect effect on educational attainment, yet the effect of this variable was relatively small and was barely larger than .05, which Land (1969) and Pedhazur (1982) recommended as the minimum effect size that was to be considered substantively important.

Eight variables were found to have significant total effects in the following order of magnitude: ability (total effect = .343), academic performance (total effect = .284), educational aspiration (total effect = .260), SES (total effect = .160), significant others' influence (total effect = .122), occupational aspiration (total effect = .131), the number of children (total effect = -.092), and sex (total effect = -.087). The negative effect for the number of children shows, perhaps it is natural, that those who have fewer children are more likely than those who have more children to attain higher levels of education. The negative effect for sex indicates that men are more likely than women to attain higher levels of education. The positive effects of the other six variables indicate that the higher the SES, ability, academic performance, significant others' influence, educational aspiration, and occupational aspiration are, the higher the educational attainment will be.

Dominant mediators for the indirect effects of SES and ability were significant others' influence, educational aspiration, academic performance, and occupational aspiration. While the mediators for the indirect influence of academic performance were significant others' influence, educational aspiration, and occupational aspiration, educational aspiration was the mediator of the indirect effect of significant others' influence. Educational aspiration was a primary mediating variable for the indirect effects of all the four variables on educational attainment.

Occupational Attainment

Eight variables had significant indirect effects on occupational attainment in the following order of magnitude (see Table 4.4): ability, academic performance, educational aspiration, SES, occupational aspiration, sex, significant others' influence, and the number of children. Although the strongest indirect effect on occupational attainment came from ability, both academic performance and educational aspiration had relatively strong indirect effects on it.

Three variables had significant total effects on occupational attainment in the following order of magnitude: educational attainment (total effect = .389); occupational aspiration (total effect = .214); and academic performance (total effect = .201). In other words, the higher these three variables are, the higher the occupational attainment will be. The effect of educational attainment was by far larger than other two variables, suggesting that educational attainment would be the most important contributor to occupational attainment on the assumption that all the other conditions are equal.

While the dominant mediators for the indirect effects of SES and academic performance were educational attainment and occupational aspiration, dominant mediators for the indirect effects of sex and ability were educational attainment, occupational aspiration, and academic performance. Indeed, educational attainment was the mediator for the indirect effects of significant others, educational aspiration, occupational aspiration, and the number of children. It should be noted that educational attainment is the dominant mediator for the indirect effects of all the eight variables on occupational attainment after all.

Finally, the emphasis in this chapter has been on a quantitative description of the results of the model estimation for the NLS-72 final sample. The estimated influences (see Figure 4.1) illustrate a visual contrast to the theorized influences (see Figure 3.1). In the following chapter, the meanings of the results are fully evaluated and interpreted, especially with respect to the original hypotheses of this study.

Table 4.3 Effects and Mediators on the Educational
Attainment Process[a]

	Direct Effects	Indirect Effects	Total Effects	Intervening Variables
SES	.107** (.036)	.053** (.018)	.160** (.054)	Significant others' influence Educational aspiration Occupational aspiration Academic performance
Sex	-.077** (-.161)	-.010 (-.021)	-.087** (-.182)	
Ability	.116** (.039)	.227** (.076)	.343** (.115)	Significant others' influence Educational aspiration Occupational aspiration Academic performance
Academic Performance	.193* (.008)	.091** (.004)	.284** (.012)	Significant others' influence Educational aspiration Occupational aspiration
Significant Others' Influence	.049* (.043)	.073** (.063)	.122* (.106)	Educational aspiration
Educational Aspiration	.260** (.275)	- -	.260** (.275)	
Occupational. Aspiration	131** (.007)	- -	.131** (.007)	
Marital Status	-.019 (-.055)	- -	-.019 (-.055)	
Number of Children	-.092** (-.086)	- -	-.092** (-.086)	

[a]Unstandardized coefficients are given in parentheses.
*$p < .01$; **$p < .001$.

Table 4.4   Effects and Mediators on the Occupational
Attainment Process[a]

	Direct Effects	Indirect Effects	Total Effects	Intervening Variables
SES	.048 (.298)	.065** (.404)	.113 (.702)	Educational attainment Occupational aspiration
Sex	-.005 (-.214)	-.046** (-1.821)	-.051 (-2.035)	Educational attainment Occupational aspiration Academic performance
Ability	.026 (.163)	.185** (1.160)	.211 (1.323)	Educational attainment Occupational aspiration Academic performance
Academic Performance	.068* (.055)	.133** (.108)	.201* (.163)	Educational attainment Occupational aspiration
Significant Others' Influence	-.043 (-.700)	.043** (.697)	.000 (-.003)	Educational attainment
Educational Aspiration	-.038 (-.760)	.101** (2.003)	.063 (1.243)	Educational attainment
Occupational Aspiration	.163** (.166)	.051** (.052)	.214** (.218)	Educational attainment
Marital Status	.008 (.451)	-.007 (-.398)	.001 (.053)	
Number of Children	-.047 (-.827)	-.036** (-.629)	-.083 (-1.456)	Educational attainment
Educational Attainment	.389** (7.278)	- -	.389** (7.278)	

[a]Unstandardized coefficients are given in parentheses.
*p < .01; **p < .001.

Chapter 5

Discussion

The first section of this chapter makes a comparison between the Wisconsin theoretical model and the estimated model of this study. The second section deals with the process of status attainment for the NLS-72 sample. The third section discusses the impacts of marriage and children on the status attainment process. In the fourth section, path analyses for this study are summarized and then concluded.

Comparisons with the Wisconsin Model

The Wisconsin model was conceptualized to investigate the attainment process for American white men, and the process was hypothesized to be a function of the cognitive-motivational component formed by aspirations and of the contextual component formed by social-psychological factors influencing attainment. As has been evident, many of the effects hypothesized to be zero by the Wisconsin model are in fact statistically significant in this study. This significance, however, may in part be due to the larger sample size used in this study ($N = 2,160$), as compared to the original Wisconsin model estimation ($N = 739$). Of particular note, this study indicates that the process is the same for men and women comprising the study sample. This is the result of the lack of interactive effects, indicating that (1) both the magnitude and (2) the direction of each effect within the model are the same for men and women. Specifically, while women have lower educational and occupational aspirations and actually attain lower education levels, (1) the relationship between aspiration and attainment and (2) the process by which aspiration and attainment are reached are both consistent for men and women in this sample.

The Wisconsin model hypothesized that the dominant effect on academic performance would be ability, with a possible effect from SES backgrounds. This study supports these hypothesized effects. In the analysis for this sample, academic performance is mostly influenced by ability. And the effect of SES on academic performance is negative and very small relative to the effect of ability; indeed, this is an unexpected result because research has indicated "a positive relationship between social origin and high school academic performance" (Hawser 1970). For this sample of students, the monetary benefits (from higher SES backgrounds) may result in those students attending more selective, challenging, and competitive high schools.

The Wisconsin model further hypothesized that the dominant effects on significant others' influence would be academic performance and SES. The results of this study partially support these hypothesized influences. Academic performance has the strongest effect, and SES has the third strongest effect on significant others' influence. Contrary to the hypothesis of the Wisconsin model, the result of this study indicates that ability has a strong direct effect, even stronger than its indirect effect, on significant others' influence. Interestingly enough, when combined with its indirect influence, ability carries the strongest impact on significant others' influence, and SES does appear much less important. It is then the student's academic performance and ability that establish the expectation of significant others rather than the SES backgrounds from which the student comes.

The Wisconsin theoretical model posits that significant others' influence is the dominant influence on educational aspiration. Although this position is substantiated for this sample, the four other variables (SES, sex, ability, and academic performance) also exert influences on educational aspiration (even though their effects are lesser in magnitude). While significant others' influence has a dominant influence on educational aspiration, parental socioeconomic backgrounds determine educational aspiration directly rather than indirectly as suggested by the Wisconsin model.

There is a considerable departure from the Wisconsin model in the pattern of influence on occupational aspiration. Contrary to the hypothesis of the Wisconsin model, the analysis for this sample indicates that significant others' influence has no direct effect on occupational aspiration. The dominant influences on occupational aspiration for this sample are such variables as sex and academic performance. In addition, there is a relatively strong effect of social origin (SES) on occupational aspiration (and on educational aspiration as well). Anyway, for this sample, SES backgrounds affect educational and occupational aspirations directly rather than indirectly through significant others' influence.

As hypothesized by the Wisconsin model, the dominant effect on educational attainment is educational aspiration. Wisconsin model posits a possible effect from significant others' influence on educational attainment; but, this is not the case in this study in which the effect is very small, even though statistically significant. For this sample both academic performance and occupational aspiration have much larger effects than does significant others' influence on educational attainment. This study also indicates that there is a continuing direct influence of social origin (much greater than its indirect influence) on educational attainment which, in turn, has the strongest influence on occupational attainment as hypothesized by the Wisconsin model. Furthermore, occupational aspiration has a direct effect, which is the second strongest influence, on occupational attainment.

In most instances the dominant effects in the variables within the model that were hypothesized by the Wisconsin model were forthcoming in this study. However, social origin did play a much larger role in influencing subsequent constructs than what was anticipated, and its influence was more direct than indirect as was hypothesized. The significant direct influence of sex on educational and occupational aspirations as well as on educational attainment indicates that even after controlling other social-psychological constructs, women still have lower educational and occupational aspirations and, of course, attain lower levels of education as well.

Lastly, the lack of the significant influence of sex on occupational attainment, however, indicates that both men and women with similar levels of occupational aspiration and educational attainment tend to attain the same occupational status.

The Status Attainment Process

The results of this study show that the strongest positive direct influence on occupational attainment comes from educational attainment, strongly supporting the premise that educational attainment is the key to occupational attainment. The results of this study further support the established notion by Haller and Portes (1973) that the influence of SES on the subsequent occupational success is indirect, albeit this indirect influence occurs chiefly through enhancing (1) educational and occupational aspirations and (2) educational attainment. Educational and occupational aspirations strongly influence education levels attained by this sample of Americans, and this findings supports Rojewski's (1996) notion that educational (and occupational) aspirations are very important precursors to the individual's status attainment.

The attainment process appears to be complex and is, in essence, a complex multivariate process. According to Sewell and Hawser (1975, 9), "The most critical factor in the process of attaining higher education is the decision to plan on and to enter college." The results of this study confirm that "to pursue or to ignore a postsecondary education" (Rojewski 1996) is a matter of great importance for high school seniors, particularly in terms of educational attainment as well as early occupational attainment. However, it is found, after considering the indirect and total effects on educational attainment, that ability and academic performance are the strongest effects. Even so, educational aspiration still arises as a primary contributor to educational attainment, strongly mediating the influences of ability and SES.

"Schools," as Hawser (1970, 102) has put it, "are primary agencies of social selection for children and youth of the United States." With such an emphasis, "Everything that happens to a boy before his sixteenth birthday influences everything that happens after that by way of his education" (Siegel, cited in Hawser 1970, 111). In more recent research (Entwisle 1993, 401), "Educational stratification begins in earnest when children start formal schooling. . . . Children who are poor very often get low test scores in school. . . . Poverty is not their only burden"; needless to say, such children are inclined to attend schools with others from disadvantaged homes and, therefore, get off to a shaky start when making the first-grade transition.

The notion that the impact of social origin is decidedly stronger on educational attainment rather than on occupational attainment is one that has considerable face validity. This study supports that validity. As a result of this analysis of the characteristics of the individual and social conditions influencing the status attainment, social origin has a direct effect on educational attainment but not on occupational attainment. In Charters's (cited in Hawser 1970) words, social-class positions predict grades, achievements, and intelligence test scores. On the contrary, in this study, low-SES students are more likely than high-SES students to demonstrate better academic performance. This result suggests, as stated before, that students from high-SES families attend better schools with more competitive student bodies. The second strongest direct effect on educational attainment comes from academic performance, supporting the finding of Pope (1972, 38): "High school rank is a well recognized predictive value for a college degree."

The impact of background characteristics (SES and ability) on educational attainment are mediated by the product of schooling (academic performance), the cognitive-motivational function (educational and occupational status aspirations), and the social-psychological support (i.e., significant others' influence) in high school days. Naturally, for this sample of Americans, ability (more than six times the effect of SES) has the strongest direct effect on academic performance, which has the second strongest direct effect on educational attainment. In short, on the assumption that "Failure to achieve in school can have negative effects on occupational success and income power" (Anderson 1993, 342), these results reported here are notable.

It does appear that the path to occupational attainment is determined by educational attainment, which is determined by educational (and occupational) aspirations. The impact of educational attainment (more than two times the direct effect of occupational aspiration and almost six times the direct effect of academic performance) on occupational attainment is not negligible. This impact does suggest a very strong linkage between educational and occupational attainment. Nearly everyone agrees that a college education is of considerable help for achieving occupational status; however, the basic fact that educational and occupational achievements are intertwined is rarely disputed. According to Spaeth and Greeley (1970), this is because many people advocate that higher education should provide students with occupational training, whereas there are many people who give higher priority to other goals, such as the intellectual or personal development of students. That is to say, understanding how strongly educational and occupational aspirations are related to educational and occupational attainment is, after all, the key to understanding the underpinning of American social structures (Woelfel 1972).

Occupational attainment is associated with not only academic performance but also SES backgrounds (Grubb 1993). This premise is supported by this study because the indirect positive influence of SES on occupational attainment is small (contrary to the hypothesis) but statistically significant. This study further supports Treiman and Terrell's (1975) theorized notion that occupational attainment is significantly dependent on educational attainment and only slightly dependent on SES backgrounds.

The dynamics of the process by which Americans attain social or occupational status, in a way, are evidenced in the strongest paths of influence forthcoming from the model for this study. Figure 5.1 illustrates the most reliable paths of status attainment for this sample: (1) ability produces academic performance; (2) both of which, in turn, establish significant others' influence; (3) occupational aspiration is strongly determined by academic performance; (4) the dominant effect on educational aspiration is from significant others' influence; (5) yet SES also strongly impacts educational and occupational aspirations; (6) educational attainment is dominantly the result of academic performance and educational aspiration; and (7) educational attainment is, in turn, the determinant of occupational attainment, even though occupational aspiration also has a strong effect on occupational attainment.

Social-psychological factors have the direct and the indirect effects of their own within the model, which are independent of SES backgrounds. SES exerts its influence directly mainly on both types of aspiration, albeit these influences on both aspirations are not the dominant ones. These results once again support Treiman and Terrell's (1975) finding that both the educational attainment process and the occupational attainment process are basically the same.

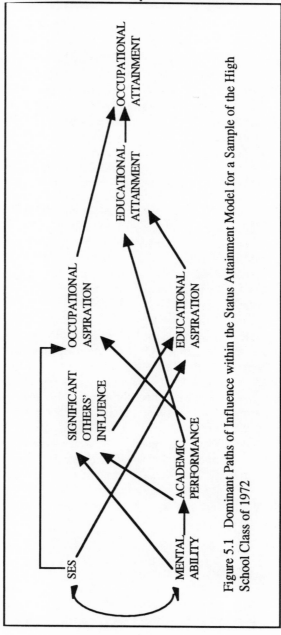

Figure 5.1 Dominant Paths of Influence within the Status Attainment Model for a Sample of the High School Class of 1972

Impacts of Marriage and Children

Marital status and the number of children (although not of principal focus but of interest for the status attainment of women) were used as control variables to accurately assess the influence of variables. According to the review of literature by Nesbitt (1995), marriage and family (spouses and children, to be exact) are consistently beneficial for and have positive effects on the occupational attainment of men. Nesbitt has further claimed that women receive benefits from marriage in terms of security and prestige, which tend to contribute to their status attainment. For this sample, marital status has neither direct nor indirect effects on educational and occupational attainment.

Instead, the results of this study support the findings of Nesbitt (1995) that (1) educational attainment is not related to marital status for men and women, and (2) married women are just as likely as single women to hold similar levels of positions at work. More important, the present results support the position that marital differences are less important than gender differences on the status attainment process for American people (Roos, cited in Nesbitt 1995).

The results of this study also support the position that the equality of male and female occupational status is not so anomalous with respect to other gender inequalities in the United States (McClendon 1976). The model estimation for this sample indicates that there is no interactive effect but that men tend to attain higher levels of education yet not higher levels of occupation when compared to women with similar social backgrounds. The model estimation for this sample also indicates that the number of children has a significant negative direct influence on educational attainment. The dual responsibility of work and home may contribute to this negative effect. In summary, like the impact of marriage, the impact of the number of children as an independent variable on the status attainment process is the same for this sample of men and women, and the impact of marriage is relatively small within the context of this model.

Summary and Conclusion

The essential question addressed in this study was whether or not the attainment process was the same for men and women, and it was found to be the same for this sample. In particular, the influence of SES is just as important for women as for men. Unlike the original Wisconsin sample, social origin in this sample has a much stronger effect directly than indirectly on the attainment process. Even so, as stated repeatedly, the key ingredient for occupational attainment is educational attainment, with educational and occupational aspirations the precursors.

The Wisconsin model has given evidence that the privilege of social origin (high-SES) on subsequent attainment levels is significantly mediated by academic performance, social influence, and status aspiration, in particular, in high school participations. This sample of men and women, however, illustrates the continuing "privilege of social origin" in the influence of SES both on educational and occupational aspirations and on educational attainment, indicating the following unusual relationship: low-SES students are more likely than high-SES students to demonstrate higher academic performance. Despite this unusual relationship, other influences manifested are reasonably consistent with the Wisconsin model. Interestingly, however, both marital status and the number of children do not differentially impact the educational and occupational attainment process for men and women.

It should be emphasized that access to American higher education has substantially changed for women with the times; thus today women constitute a higher proportion of the undergraduate population than men in the United States. The results of this model estimation punctuate the paradox of women's attainment: specifically, in spite of the fact that women's high school academic performance is superior to that of men, not only women have lower levels of both educational and occupational aspirations than do men, but also women's educational attainment levels are lesser than men's.

Most important, this study provides considerable evidence that "both the development and the maintenance of status aspirations" (Sewell and Hawser 1980) in high school experiences, indeed, exert pronounced influences on the probability of an individual's success in the adult and occupational world. Aspiration itself is not necessarily an indicator of eventual attainment but does play a vital role in identifying and seizing future opportunities. In short, the theory and the data in this study strongly agree that educational and occupational aspirations are both possible precursors. As regards status aspiration, the results of this study have also revealed that significant others' influence has a direct effect on educational aspiration (which, in turn, has the strongest influence on educational attainment), clarifying a very strong association of significant others' influence (that is, parents' and teachers' encouragement and support for setting higher educational and occupational goals) with educational aspiration.

The results of this study could be applied to today's American adolescents for two major reasons. One reason is that the attainment process in the model estimation of this study is found to be similar for men and women. The other is that the attainment process of the model estimation for 1972 high school graduates is found to be similar to that of the initial Wisconsin model estimation for 1957 high school graduates. Accordingly, these consistencies of the present results suggest (1) that the attainment process is still the same for American adolescents and (2) that the importance of educational aspiration is still the determinant of educational attainment for American adolescents.

As one practical implication of this research, the results can be used for enhanced academic and career education and for counseling adolescents in the transition from high school to the adult and occupational world who often need help in setting educational and occupational goals. In other words, the above-mentioned consistencies underscore the need particularly for parents, teachers, and school counselors to encourage as well as to assist students in the early years of schooling so that they are able to set attainable academic and social goals. It should be emphasized that despite the fact that educational aspiration for the sample of this study was measured in the respondent's senior year of high school, there was a strong influence of significant others on educational aspiration. This strong influence might be equally important perhaps in the earlier years of schooling.

Finally, as McCormick has stated, "It is surprising, but little is known about how students' educational aspirations change as they mature and gain experience in the educational and occupational worlds" (1997, 1) In this regard, this book, which was documented based on path analysis of a national sample, is such an indication of the importance of adolescents' educational ambitions (and related variables) in their educational and occupational attainment.

References

Adelman, C. 1992. W*omen at Thirty Something: Paradoxes of Attainment.* Washington, D.C.: U.S. Department of Education.

Airsman, L. A. 1993. "A Comparative Study of the Occupational Attainment Processes of White Men and Women in the United States." *Journal of Comparative Family Studies.* 24: 171-187.

Alexander, K. L., B. K. Eckland, and L. J. Griffin. 1975. "The Wisconsin Model of Socioeconomic." *American Journal of Sociology.* 81: 324-342.

Alwin, D. F., L. B. Otto, and V. R. A. Call. 1976. "The Schooling Process in the Development of Aspirations: A Replication." Unpublished Paper, Indiana University.

American Council on Education. 1989. *Fact Book on Women in Higher Education (1989-1990).* New York: MacMillan.

Anderson, K. H. 1993. "The Effect of Deviance During Adolescence on the Choice of Jobs." *Southern Economic Journal.* 60: 341-356.

Astin, A. W. 1993. *What Matters in College?: Four Critical Years Revisited.* San Francisco: Jossey-Bass.

Baird, L. L. 1976. "Who Goes to Graduate Schools and How They Get There." *Scholars in the Making: The Development of Graduate and Professional Students.* Edited by J. Katz and R. T. Hartneit. Cambridge, MA: Ballinger.

Bank, B. J. 1995. "Gendered Accounts: Undergraduates Explain Why They Seek Their Bachelor's Degree." *Sex Roles: A Journal of Research.* 32: 527-544.

Biniaminov, I, and N. S. Glasman. 1983. "School Determinants of Student Achievement in Secondary Education." *American Educational Research Journal.* 20: 251-268.

Blau, P. M., and O. D. Duncan. 1967. *The American Occupational Structure.* New York: Wiley.

Blau, P. M., ed. 1975. *Approaches to the Study of Social Structure.* New York: Free Press.

Blocher, D. H., and R.S. Rapoza. 1988. "Professional and Vocational Preparations." *The Modern American College.* Edited by A. W. Chickering, 212-255. San Francisco: Jossey-Bass.

Bolig, R. A. 1982. "The Ambivalent Decision." *The Ph.D. Experience:*

A Woman's Point of View. Edited by S. Vartuli, 5-26. New York: Praeger Publishers.

Breiger, R. L. 1995. "Social Structure and the Phenomenology of Attainment." *Annual Review of Sociology Annual.* 21:115-136.

Cabrera, A. F., A. Nora, and N. B. Castaneda. 1993. "College Persistence: Structural Equations Modeling Test of an Integrated Model of Student Retention." *Journal of Higher Education.* 64: 123-139.

Carrigan, S. D. 1995. "Comparisons of Women's Colleges and Coed Colleges: A Review of Literature." Paper presented at the Annual Meeting of the Mid-South Educational Research Association, Biloxi, MS.

Coll, F., and M. Coll. 1993. *Baccalaureate Origins of Doctorate Recipients: A Ranking by Discipline of 4-year Private Institutions.* ERIC Document Reproduction Service No. ED 356 705.

Congressional Quarterly Service. 1965. *Congress and the Nation (1945-1964).* Washington, D.C.: Congressional Quarterly Service.

Corcoran, M. 1980. "Sex Differences in Measurement Error in Status Attainment Models." *Sociological Methods & Research.* 9: 199-217.

Crouse, J., and P. Mueser. 1978. "Young Men's Socioeconomic Achievement in the United States." Unpublished Monograph. University of Chicago.

Dobriner, W. M. 1969. *Social Structures and Systems: A Sociological Overview.* Pacific Palisades, CA: Goodyear.

Duncan, O. D. 1961. "A Socioeconomic Index for all Occupations." *Occupations and Social Status."* Edited by A. J. Reiss, 109-138. New York: Free Press.

Duran, B. J., and R. E. Weffer. 1992. "Immigrants' Aspirations, High School Process, and Academic Outcomes." *American Educational Research Journal.* 29:163-181.

Einstein, B. W. 1967. *Guide to Success in College.* New York: Grosset and Dunlap.

Entwisle, D. R. 1993. "Entry Into School: The Beginning School Transition and Educational Stratification in the United States." *Annual Review of Sociology Annual.* 19:401-423.

Ethington, C. A., and J. C. Smart. 1986. "Persistence to Graduate

Education." *Research in Higher Education.* 24: 287-303.

Ethington, C. A., J. C. Smart, and E. T. Pascarella. 1991. "Influences on Women's Entry into Male-Dominated Occupations." *Women's Higher Education in Comparative Perspective.* Edited by G. P. Kelly and S. Slaughter, 201-218. Netherlands: Kluwer Academic Publishers.

Ethington, C. A. 1992. "Gender Differences in a Psychological Model of Mathematics Achievement." *Journal for Research in Mathematics Education.* 23: 166-181.

Feagin, J. R. 1996. Review of *Facing up to the American Dream: Race, Class, and the Soul of the Nation.* American Political Science Review. 90: 429-430.

Feldman, S. D. 1974. *Escape from the Doll's House: Women in Graduate and Professional School Education.* New York: McGraw-Hill.

Franklin, M. 1995. "The Effects of Differential College Environments on Academic Learning and Student Perceptions of Cognitive Development." *Research in Higher Education.* 36: 127-153.

Gilbert, S. 1977. Education, Change, and Society: A Sociology of Canadian Education. Edited by R. A. Carlton, L. A. Colley, and N. J. Mackinon, 281. Toronto: Gage Educational Publishing.

Greene, R. G. 1995. "Graduate Education: Adapting to Current Realities." *Issues in Science and Technology.* 12: 59-66.

Griffiths, P. A. 1995. "Reshaping Graduate Education." *Issues in Science and Technology.* 11: 74-79.

Grubb, W. N. 1993. "The Varied Economic Returns to Postsecondary Education: New Evidence from the Class of 1972." *Journal of Human Resources.* 28: 365-382.

Haller, A. O., and A. Portes. 1973. "Status Attainment Process." *Sociology of Education.* 46: 51-91.

Hanson, S. 1994. "Lost Talent: Unrealized Educational Aspirations and Expectations Among U.S. Youths." *Sociology of Education.* 67: 159-183.

Hawser, R. M. 1970. "Education Stratification in the United States." *Sociological Inquiry.* 40: 102-129.

Hawser, R. M., S. L. Tsai, and W.H. Sewell. 1983. "A Model of Stratification with Response Error in Social and Psychological Variables." *Sociology of Education.* 56: 20-46.

Hayes, P. S. B. 1986. *Transitions: A Study of Changing Patterns in the Lives of Adult Women Students.* Ph.D. diss., University of Alabama, 1983. University Microfilms International. No. 8401230.

Hearn, J. C. 1987. "Impacts of Undergraduate Experiences on Aspirations and Plans for Graduate and Professional Education." *Research in Higher Education.* 27: 119-141

Helen Dwight Reid Educational Foundation. 1995. "Climbing the Ladder of Success: Post-high School Performance in the Labor market." *Change.* 27: 45-48.

Henschen, B. M. 1993. "Easing the Transition from Doctoral Student to Academic Professional." *Political Science and Politics.* 26: 81-83.

Kalmijn, M. 1994. "Mother's Occupational Status and Children's Schooling." *American Sociological Review.* 59: 257-275.

Keith, T. Z., P. L. Harrison, and S.W. Ehly. 1987. "Effects of Adaptive Behavior on Achievement: Path Analysis of a National Sample." *Professional School Psychology.* 2: 205-215.

Keith, T. Z. 1988. "Path Analysis: An Introduction for School Psychologists." *School Psychology Review.* 17: 343-362.

Kerckhoff, A. C., and J. L. Huff. 1974. "Parental Influence on Educational Goals." *Sociometry.* 37: 307-327.

Kerckhoff, A. C., and R. T. Campbell. 1977. "Black-White Differences in the Educational Attainment Process." *Sociology of Education.* 50: 15-27.

Kim, M. 1995. "Women-Only College: Some Unanticipated Consequences." *Journal of Higher Education.* 66: 641-669.

Lampard, R. 1995. "Parents' Occupations and Their Children's Occupational Attainment: A Contribution to the Debate on the Class Assignment of Families." *Sociology.* 29: 715-729.

Lamport, M. A. 1993. "Student-Faculty Informal Interaction and the Effect on College Student Outcomes: A Review of the Literature." *Adolescence.* 28: 971-990.

Land, K. C. 1969. "Principle of Path Analysis." *Sociological Methodology.* Edited by E. F. Borgalta. San Francisco: Jossey-Bass.

Leatherman, C. "Survey Shows Continued Growth in Number of Science Ph.D.'s." *The Chronicle of Higher Education,* 8

December 1995, A18.

Ledman, R. 1995. "Successful Women and Women's Colleges: Is There an Intervening Variable in the Reported Relationship." *Sex Roles: A Journal of Research.* 33: 489-497.

Levine, D. O. 1979. *The condition of women in higher education: A decade of progress, an uncertain future.* ERIC Document Reproduction Service. No. 184 447.

Liao, T. F., and Y. Cai. 1995. "Socialization, Life Situations, and Gender-Role Attitudes Regarding the Family Among White American Women." *Sociological Perspectives.* 38: 241-260.

Marini, M. M. 1978. "The Transition to Adulthood: Sex Differences in Educational Attainment and Age at Marriage." *American Sociological Review.* 43: 483-507.

McClendon, M. J. 1976. "The Occupational Status Attainment Processes of Males and Females." *American Sociological Review.* 41: 52-64.

McCormick, A. C. 1997. "Changes in Educational Aspirations After High School: The Role of Postsecondary Attendance and Context." Paper presented at the Annual Meeting of the Association for the Study of Higher Education, Albuquerque, New Mexico.

National Center for Educational Statistics (NCES). 1975. *National Longitudinal Study of the High School Class of 1972: Student Questionnaire and Test Results by Sex, High School Program, Ethnic Category, and Father's Education.* Washington, D.C.: U.S. Government Printing Office.

National Center for Educational Statistics (NCES). 1976. *A Capsule Description of First Follow-Up Survey Data.* Washington, D.C.: U.S. Government Printing Office.

National Center for Educational Statistics (NCES). 1977. *National Longitudinal Study of the High School Class of 1972 - Sample Design Efficiency Study.* Washington, D.C.: U.S. Government Printing Office.

National Center for Educational Statistics (NCES). 1981. *National Longitudinal Study: Base Year (1972) Through Fourth Follow-Up (1979) Data File Users Manual.* Washington, D.C.: U.S. Department of Education.

National Center for Education Statistics (NCES). 1988. *A Descriptive Summary of 1972 High School Seniors: Fourteen Years Later.*

Washington, D.C.: U.S. Department of Education.

Nesbitt, P. D. 1995. "Marriage, Parenthood, and the Ministry: Differential Effects of Marriage and Family on Male and Female Clergy Careers." *Sociology of Religion.* 56: 397-415.

Orr, E. 1995. "Actual and Perceived Parental Social Status: Effects on Adolescent Self-Concept." *Adolescence.* 30: 603-616.

Page, E. B., and T. Z. Keith. 1981. (August/September). "Effects of U.S. Private Schools: A Technical Analysis of Two Recent Claims." *Educational Researcher,* 7-23.

Pascarella, E. T., and P. T. Terenzini. 1980. "Predicting Freshman Persistence and Voluntary Dropout Decisions from a Theoretical Model." *Journal of Higher Education.* 51: 60-75.

Pedhazur, E. J. 1982. *Multiple Regression in Behavioral Research.* New York: Holt, Rinehart, and Winston.

Picou, J. S., and T. M. Carter. 1976. "Significant-Other Influence and Aspiration." *Sociology of Education.* 49: 12-22.

Pope, R. V. 1972. *Factors Affecting the Elimination of Women Students.* New York: AMS Press.

Porter, J. N. 1974. "Race, Socialization and Mobility in Educational and Early Occupational Attainment." *American Sociological Review.* 39: 303-316.

Porter, J. N. 1976. "Socialization and Mobility in Educational and Early Occupational Attainment." *Sociology of Education.* 49: 23-33.

Reeves, S. 1994. A Burst of Popularity. *U.S. News & World Report.* 117: 105-108.

Riordan, C. 1994. "The Value of Attending a Women's College: Education, Occupation, and Income Benefits." *Journal of Higher Education.* 65: 486-510.

Rojewski, J. W. 1996. "Educational and Occupational Aspirations of High School Seniors with Learning Disabilities." *Exceptional Children.* 62: 463-476.

Roos, P., and K. W. Jones. 1993. "Shifting Gender Boundaries: Women's Inroads Into Academic Sociology." *Work and Occupations.* 20: 395-423.

Rothstein, D. S. 1995. "Do Female Faculty Influence Female Students' Educational and Labor Market Attainments?" *Industrial and Labor Relations Review.* 48: 515-530.Sander, W., and A. C. Krautmann. 1995. "Catholic Schools, Dropout Rates and

Educational Attainment." *Economic Inquiry.* 33: 217-223.

Sander, W., and A. C. Krautmann. 1995. "Catholic School, Dropout Rates and Educational Attainment." *Economic Inquiry.* 33: 217-223.

Seltzer, R. "College Award Record Number of Ph.D.s." *Chemical & Engineering News,* 13 March 1995, 9.

Sewell, W. H., A. O. Haller, and A. Portes. 1969. "The Educational and Early Occupational Attainment Process." *American Sociological Review.* 34: 82-92.

Sewell, W. H., A. O. Haller, and G. W. Ohlendorf. 1970. "The Educational and Early Occupational Attainment: Replication and Revision." *American Sociological Review.* 35: 1014-1027.

Sewell, W. H. 1971. "Inequality of Opportunity for Higher Education." *American Sociological Review.* 36: 793-809.

Sewell, W. H., and R. M. Hawser. 1975. *Education, Occupation, and Earnings: Achievement in the Early Career.* New York: Academic Press.

Sewell, W. H., and R. M. Hawser. 1980. "The Wisconsin Longitudinal Study of Social and Psychological Factors in Aspirations and Achievement." *Research in Sociology of Education and Socialization.* 1: 59-99.

Smart, J. C. 1986. "College Effects on Occupational Status Attainment." *Research in Higher Education.* 24: 73-95.

Smith, D. G., D. E. Morrison, and L.E. Wolf. 1994. "College as a Gendered Experience: An Empirical Analysis Using Multiple Lenses." *Journal of Higher Education.* 65: 696-725.

Smith, D. G., L. E. Wolf, and D. E. Morrison. 1995. "Paths to Success: Factors Related to the Impact of Women's College." *Journal of Higher Education.* 66: 245-266.

Sobel, M. E. 1982. "Asymptotic Confidence Intervals for Indirect Effects in Structural Equation Models." *Sociological Methodology.* Edited by S. Leinhardt, 290-312. San Francisco: Jossey-Bass.

Solomon, B. M. 1985. *In the Company of Educated Women: A history of Women and Higher Education in America.* New Haven: Yale University Press.

Spaeth, M.G., and A. M. Greeley. 1970. *Recent Alumni and Higher Education.* New York: McGraw-Hill.

Spurr, S. H. 1970. *Academic Degree Structures: Innovative Approaches.* New York: McGraw-Hill.

Stoecker, J. L., and E. T. Pascarella. 1991. "Women's Colleges and Women's Career Attainments Revisited." *Journal of Higher Education.* 62: 394-411.

Syverson, P. D., and S. R. Welch. 1993. *Graduate enrollment and degrees: 1986 to 1991.* ERIC Document Reproduction Service No. ED 358 785.

Terenzini, P. T., and E. T. Pascarella. 1978. "The Relation of Students' Precollege Characteristics and Freshman Year Experience to Voluntary Attrition." *Research in Higher Education.* 9: 347-366.

Thurgood, D. H., and J. M. Weinman. 1991. *Summary Report 1990: Doctorate Recipients from United States Universities.* Washington, D.C.: National Academy Press.

Tidball, E. M. 1985. "Baccalaureate Origins of Entrants into American Medical School." *Journal of Higher Education.* 56: 385-402.

Tidball, E. M. 1986. "Baccalaureate Origins of Recent Natural Science Doctorates." *Journal of Higher Education.* 57: 606-620.

Tinto, V. 1975. "Dropout from Higher Education: A Theoretical Synthesis of Recent Research." *Review of Educational Research.* 45: 89-125.

Tittle, C. K., and E. R. Denker. 1980. *Returning Women Students in Higher Education.* New York: Praeger.

Townsend, B. K., and S. O. Mason. 1990. "Career Paths of Graduates of Higher Education Doctoral Programs." *The Review of Higher Education.* 14: 63-81.

Treiman, D. J., and K. Terrell. 1975. "Sex and the Process of Status Attainment: A Comparison of Working Women and Men." *American Sociological Review.* 40: 174-200.

Updegraff, K. A. 1996. "Gender Roles in Marriage: What Do They Mean for Girls' and Boys' School Achievement." *Journal of Youth and Adolescence.* 25: 78-88.

U.S. Department of Labor. 1991. "Chart: Women Will Earn More Doctoral Degree Than Men by the Year 2001." *Occupational Outlook Quarterly.* 35: 40.

Wilson, K. L., and A. Portes. 1975. "The Educational Attainment Process: Result from a National Sample." *American Journal of Sociology.* 81: 343-362.

Woelfel, J. 1972. "Significant Others and Their Role Relationships to Students in a High School Population." *Rural Sociology*. 37: 86-97.

Wolfle, L. M. 1985. "Applications of Causal Models in Higher Education." *Higher Education: Handbook of Theory and Research*. Edited by J. S. Smart, 381-413. New York: Agathon Press.

Wolfle, L. M., and C. A. Ethington. 1985. "GEMINI: Program for Analysis of Structural Equations with Standard Errors of Indirect Effects." *Behavior Research Methods, Instrument, and Computers*. 17: 581-584.

Zweigenhaft, R. L. 1993. "Prep School and Public School Graduates of Harvard: A longitudinal Study of the Accumulation of Social and Cultural Capital." *Journal of Higher Education*. 64: 211-225.

Appendix A

The Description of the NLS Test Battery[a]

Each student in the 1972 base-year survey was asked to complete a test battery (their estimates of reliability ranged from .78 to .90) producing scores in the following areas:

Vocabulary (15 items, 5 minutes). A brief test using synonym format. The items were selected to avoid academic or collegiate bias and to be of an appropriate level of difficulty for the twelfth grade population. Score range: 0-15.

Reading (20 items, 15 minutes). A test based on short passages (100-200 words) with related questions concerning a variety of reading skills but focusing on straightforward comprehension. In combination with the vocabulary test, it provides a means to derive a verbal score which can allow links to the normative data available for SAT. Score range: 0-20.

Letter groups (25 items, 15 minutes). A test of inductive reasoning requiring drawing general concepts from sets of data and try out hypotheses in a nonverbal context. The items consist of five groups of letters among which four group share a common characteristics while the fifth group differs. The student indicates which group differs from the others. Score rang: 0-25.

Mathematics (25 items, 15 minutes). Quantitative comparisons in which the student indicates which of two quantities is greater, or asserts their equality is greater. This type of item is relatively quickly answered and provides measurement of basic competence in mathematics. Score range: 0-25.

---

[a]Due to the proprietary nature of the test items, a copy of this instrument has not been provided (NCES 1981, 17-18).

INDEX

Note: Some entries that appear throughout this book (such as Blau-Duncan Model, Wisconsin Model, Direct Effect, Indirect Effect, Independent Variable, Dependent Variable, Educational Aspiration, Educational Attainment, Occupational Aspiration, Occupational Attainment, Parental Socioeconomic Status or SES, and Status Attainment Process) are not listed in this index.